snug.

Also by Catana Chetwynd

Little Moments of Love

snug

a collection of comics about dating your best friend

Catana Chetwynd

Andrews McMeel
PUBLISHING®

For Nana,
Her Nanliness.
Thank you for giving me my love for art.
And for everything else.

INTRODUCTION

Sometimes, we are so content in our relationship that we don't stop to think about why. It's not *particularly* because of the coffee you shared yesterday, that inside joke you laughed at together, or the kiss you got this morning, but at the same time—it is. There is something so poignantly sentimental about the moments that mean both nothing and everything. And something even more sentimental about these moments being shared between a pair of best friends.

We hope that reading this book brings a smile to your face and maybe even a quick "look" in the direction of your significant other. You know the look I'm talking about.

Remember this book was inspired by you, written for you, and exists because of people like you. We hope you see yourself in it.

So get yourself a coffee, or a glass of wine, or a nice blanket. Get snug. And enjoy this book!

snug.

catana comics

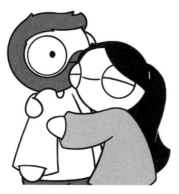

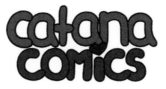

John Problems

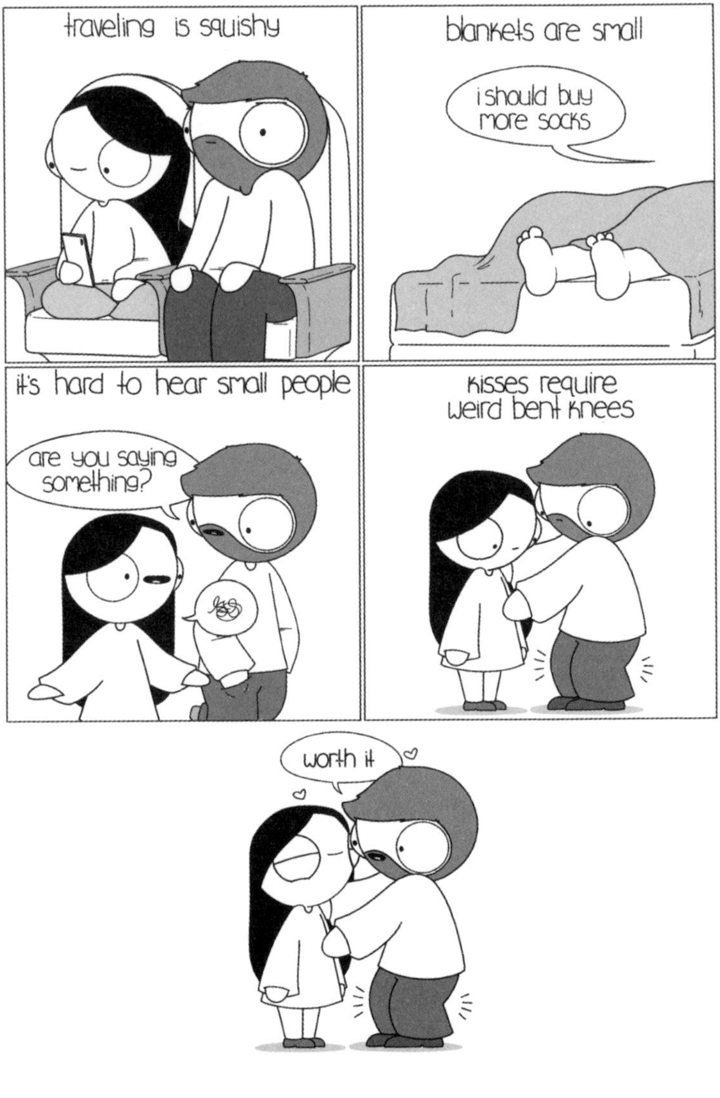
traveling is squishy
blankets are small
i should buy more socks
it's hard to hear small people
are you saying something?
kisses require weird bent knees
worth it

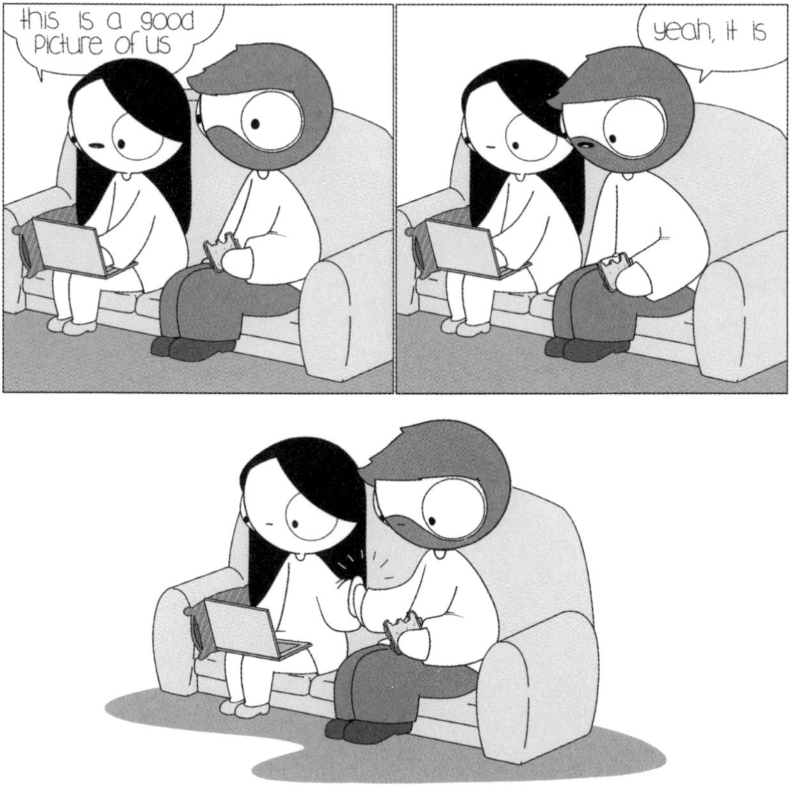
this is a good picture of us
yeah, it is

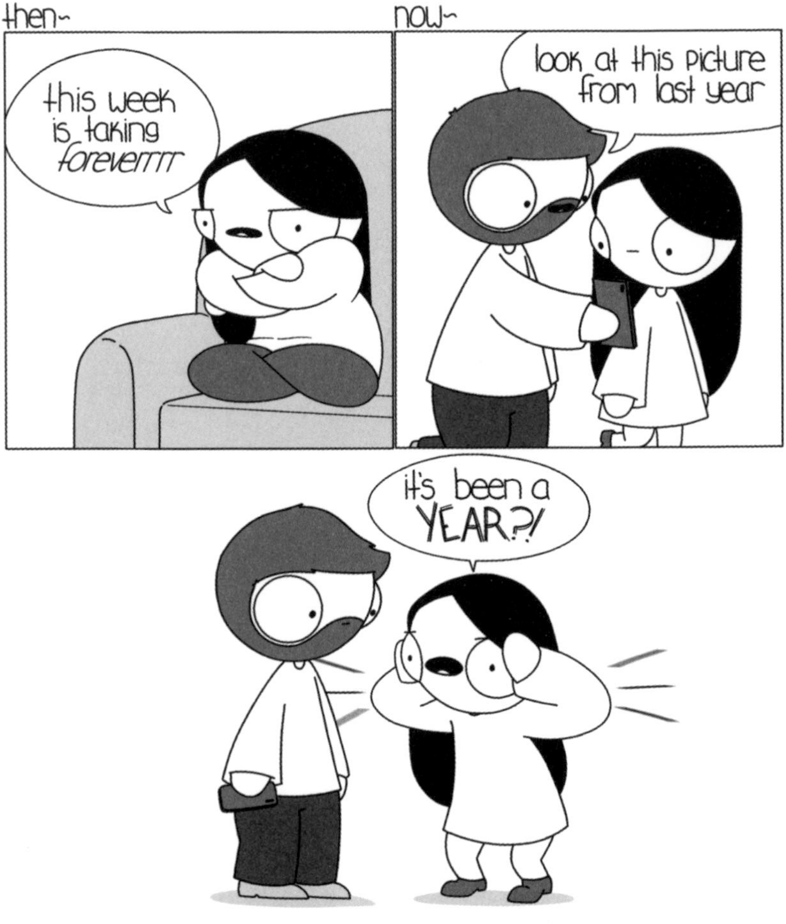
then~
this week is taking foreverrrr
now~
look at this picture from last year
it's been a YEAR?!

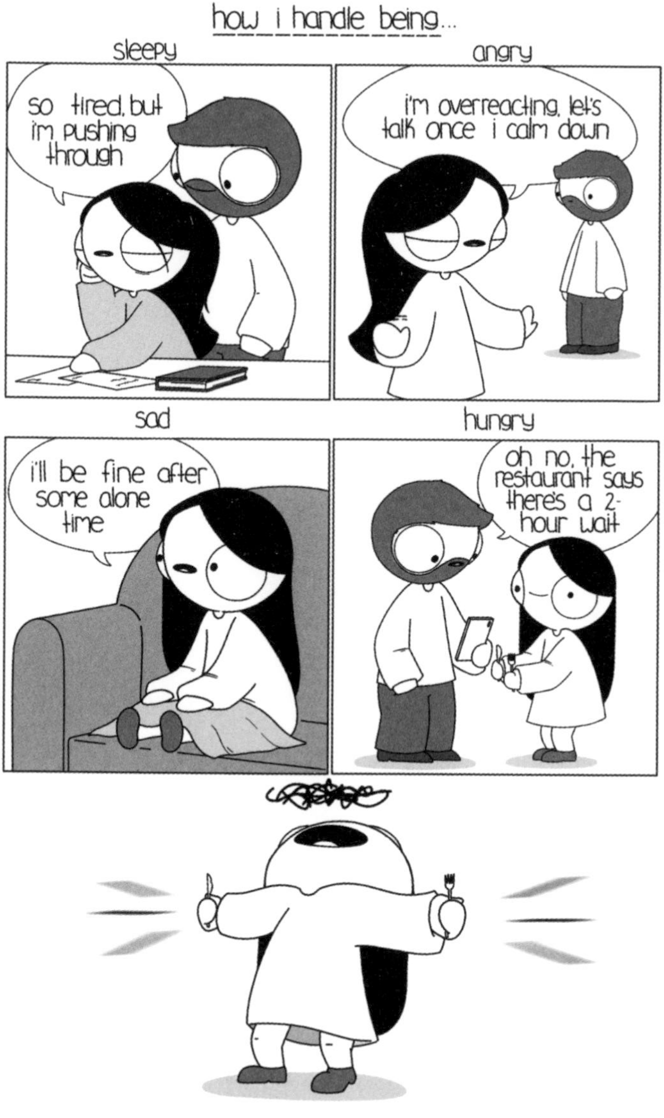
how i handle being...
sleepy
so tired, but i'm pushing through
angry
i'm overreacting, let's talk once i calm down
sad
i'll be fine after some alone time
hungry
oh no, the restaurant says there's a 2-hour wait

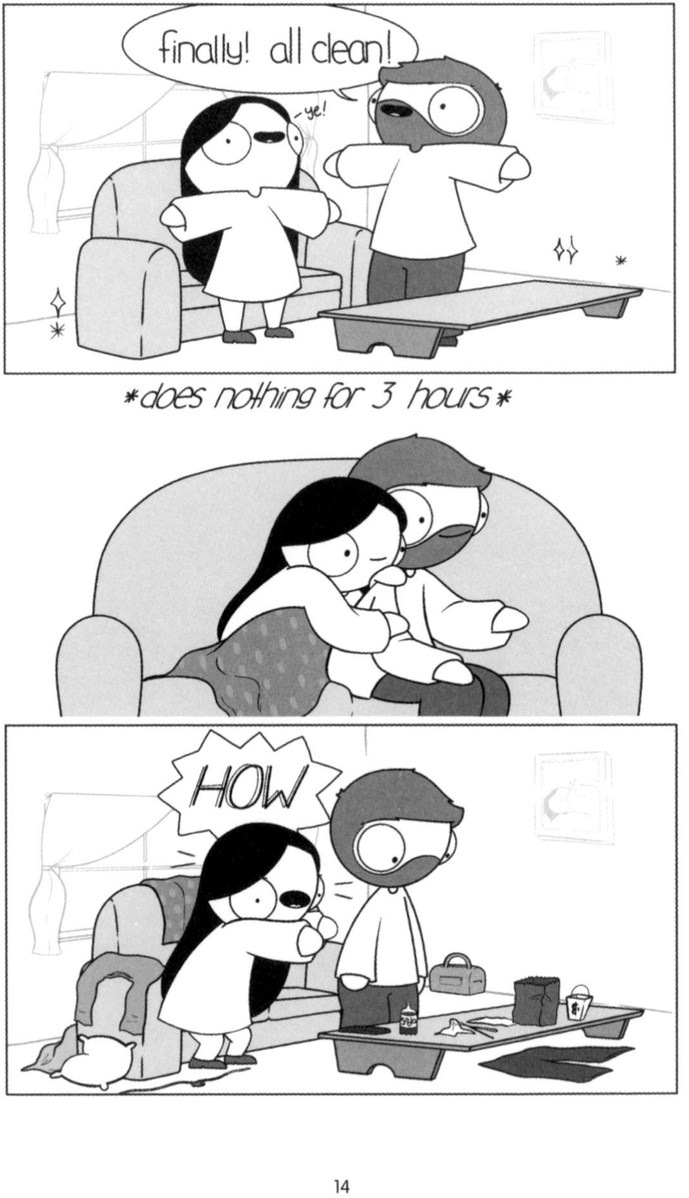
finally! all clean!
-ye!
does nothing for 3 hours
HOW

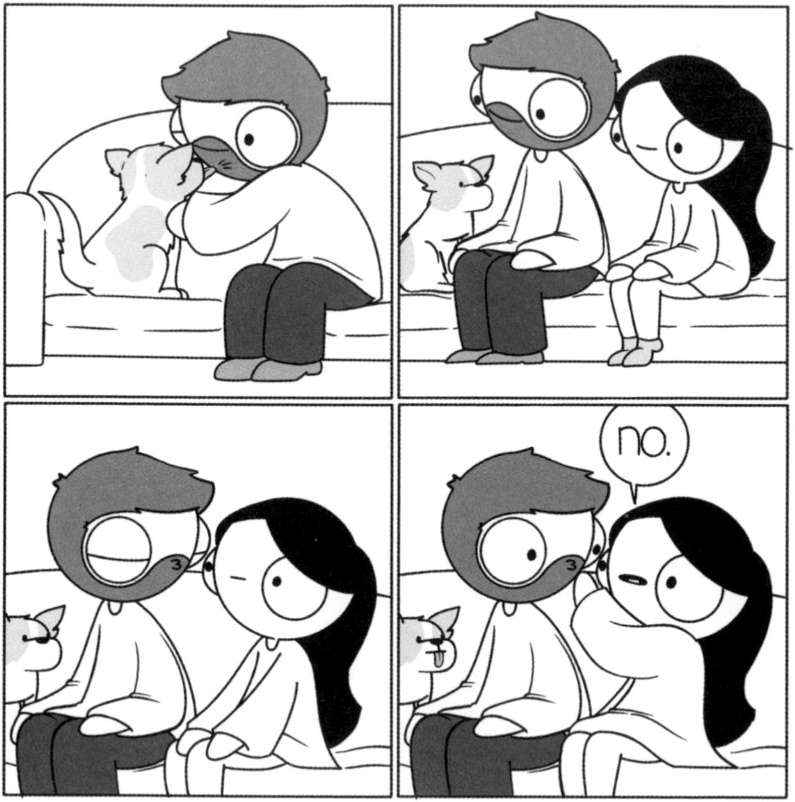
no.

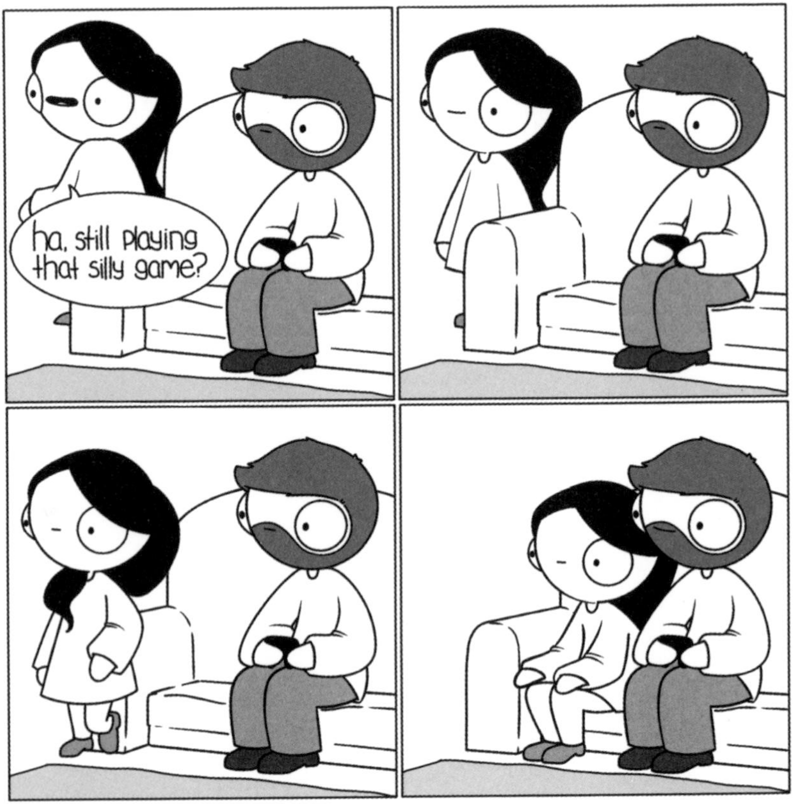
ha, still playing that silly game?

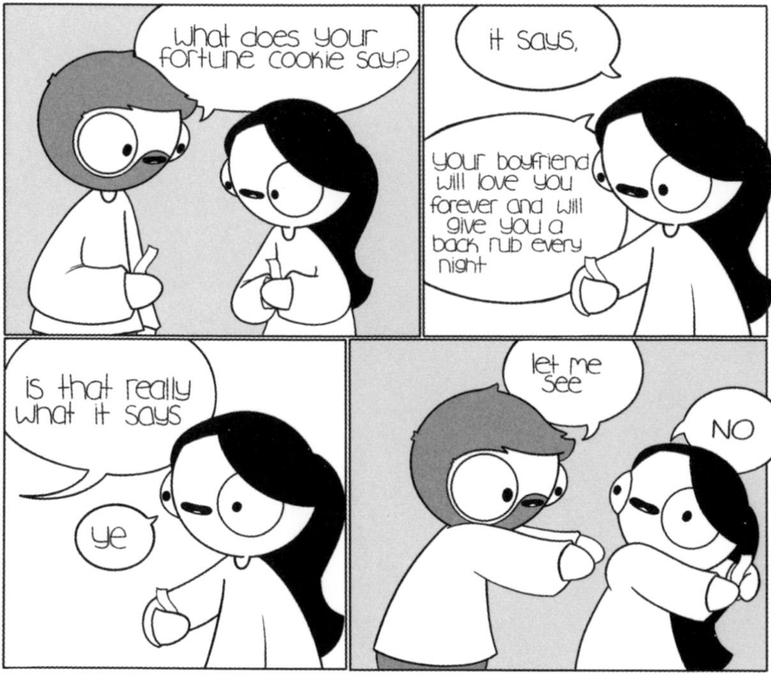
what does your fortune cookie say?
it says,
your boyfriend will love you forever and will give you a back rub every night
is that really what it says
ye
let me see
NO

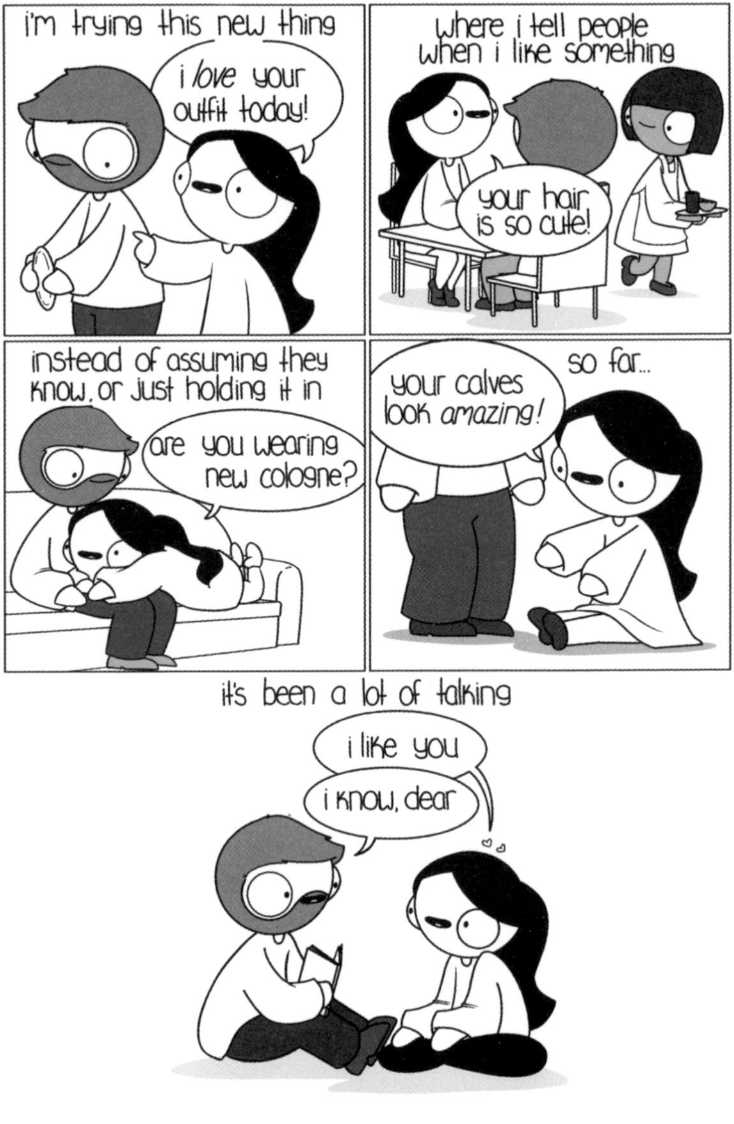

i'm trying this new thing
i *love* your outfit today!
where i tell people when i like something
your hair is so cute!
instead of assuming they know, or just holding it in
are you wearing new cologne?
so far...
your calves look *amazing*!
it's been a lot of talking
i like you
i know, dear

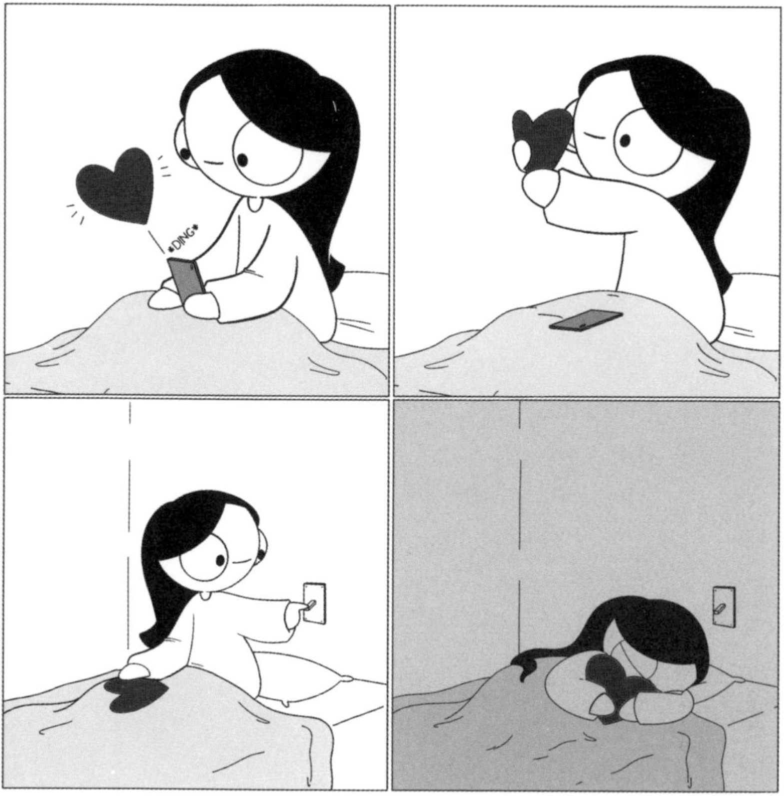
DING

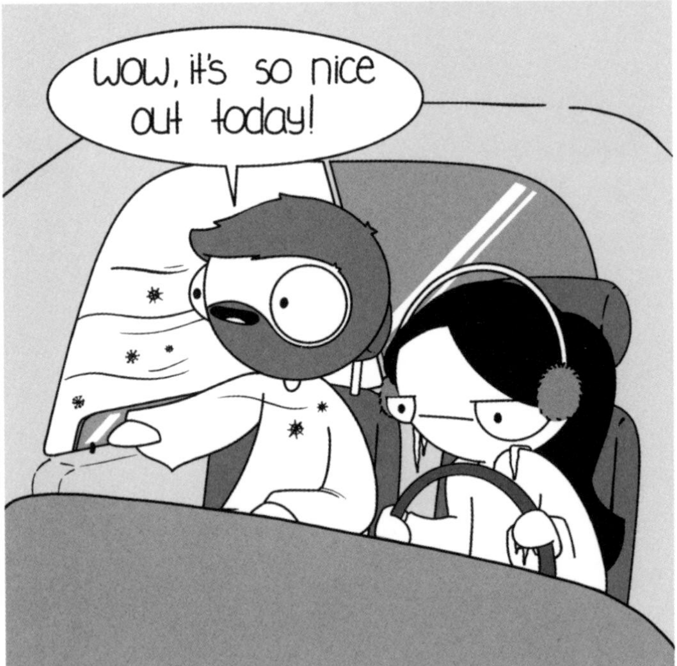
Wow, it's so nice out today!

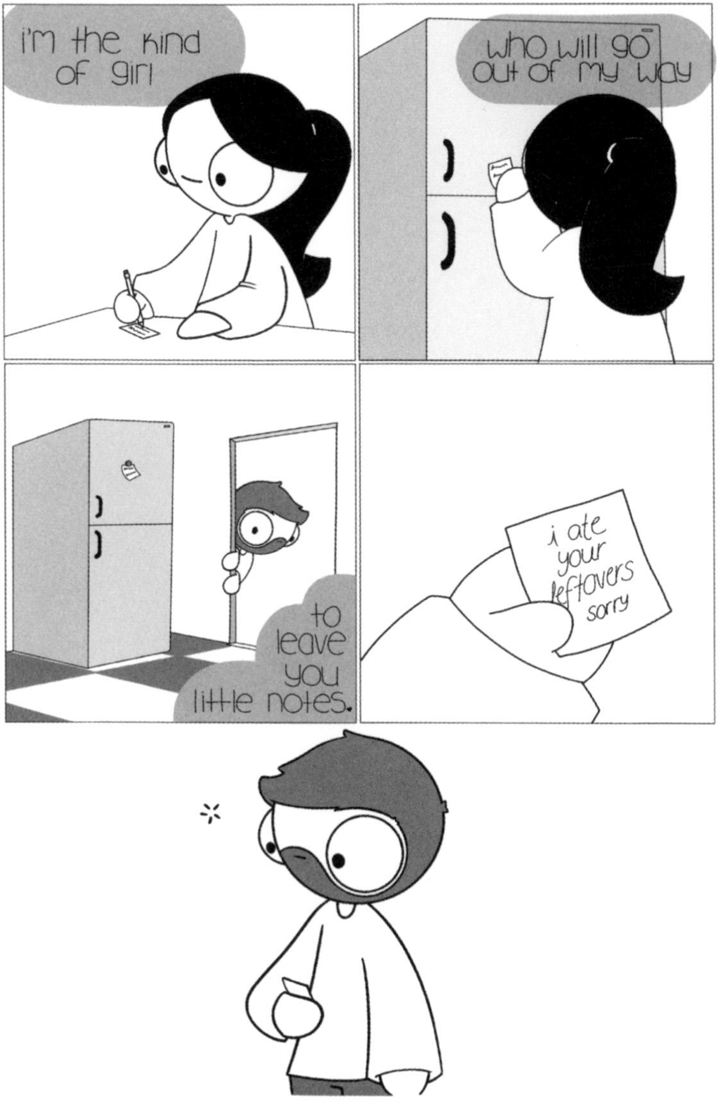
i'm the kind of girl
who will go out of my way
to leave you little notes.
i ate your leftovers sorry

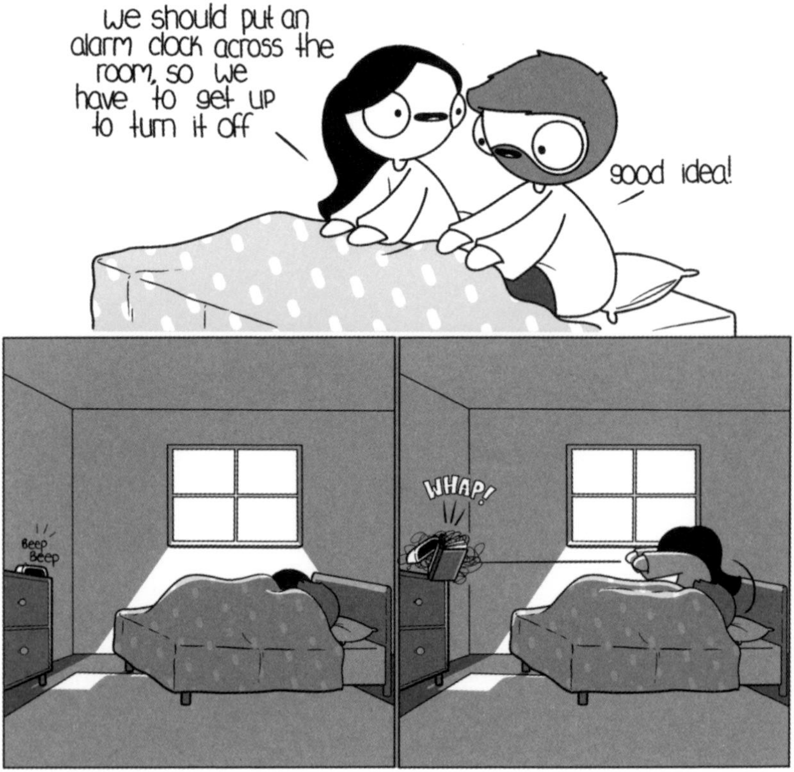
we should put an alarm clock across the room, so we have to get up to turn it off
good idea!
Beep Beep
WHAP!

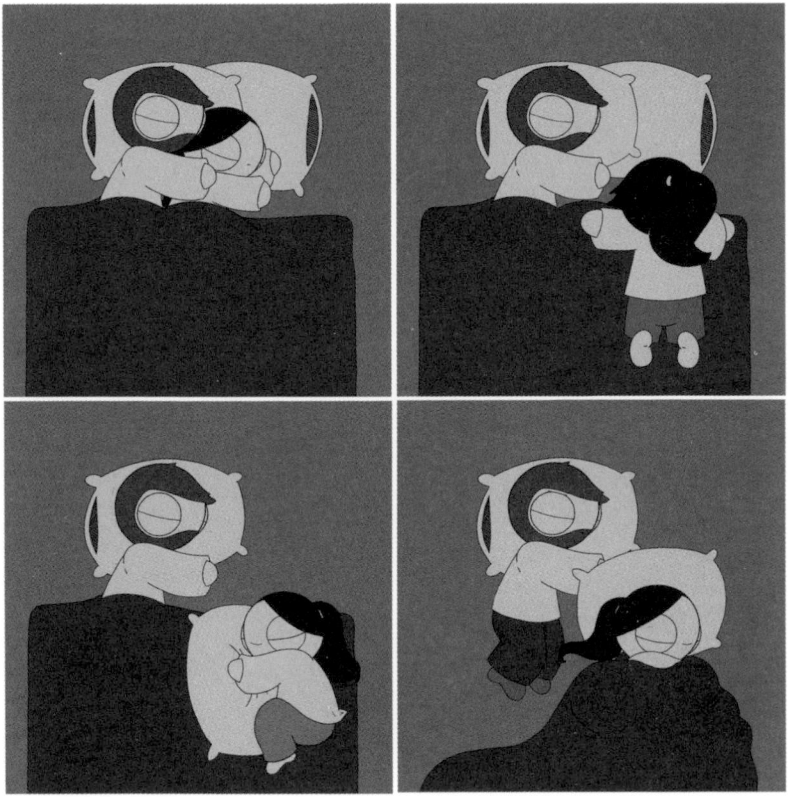

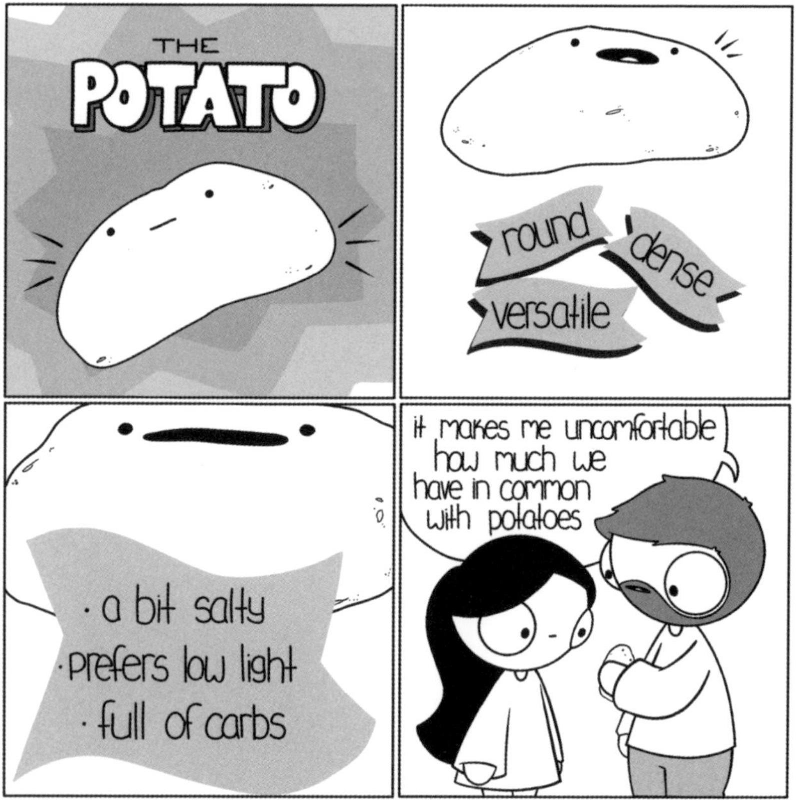
THE
POTATO
round
dense
versatile
· a bit salty
· prefers low light
· full of carbs
it makes me uncomfortable how much we have in common with potatoes

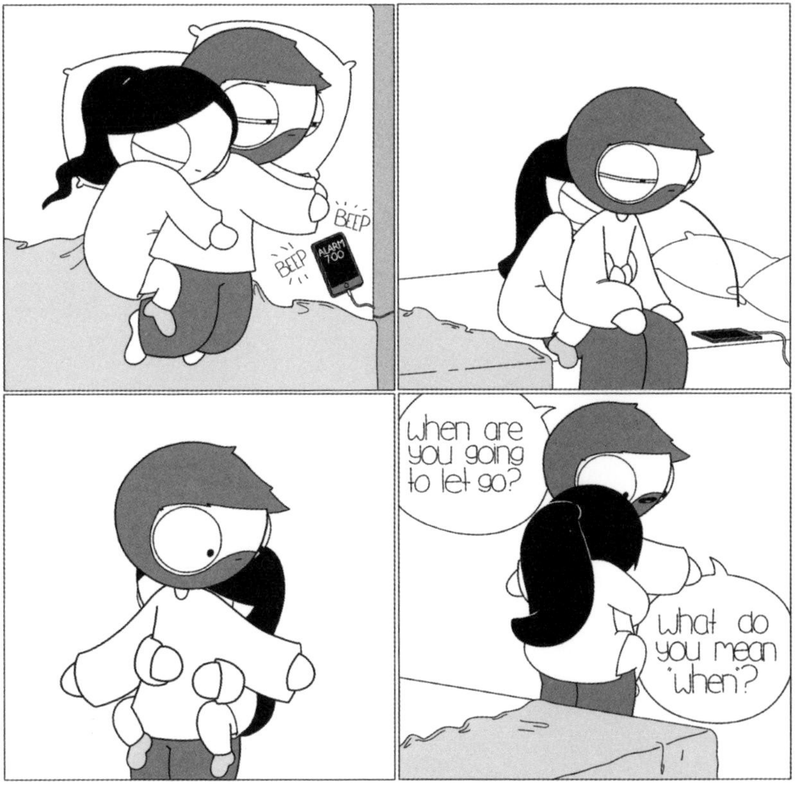
BEEP
BEEP
ALARM 7:00
When are you going to let go?
What do you mean "when"?

ordering your girlfriend's coffee

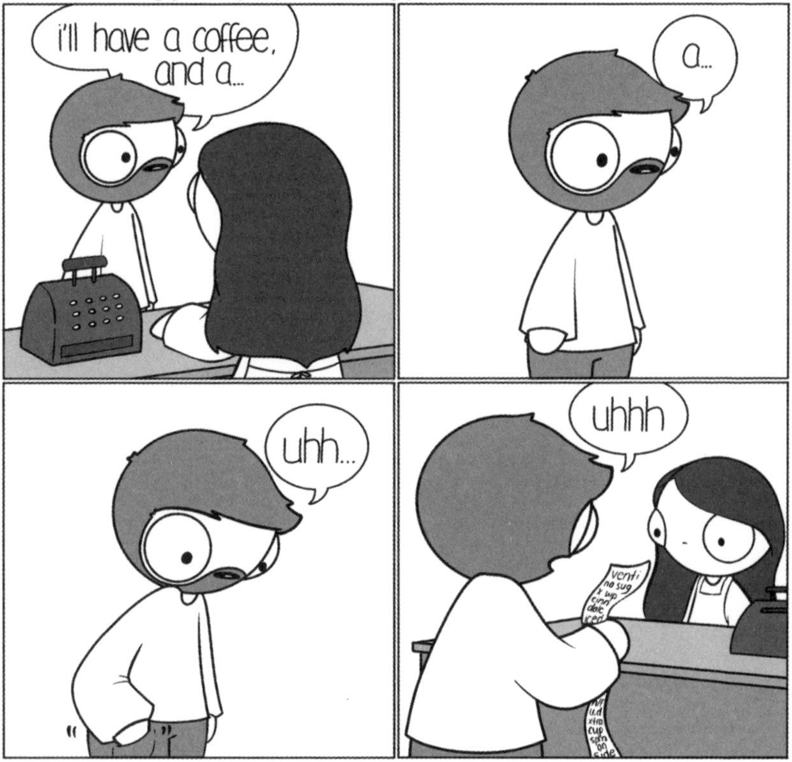
i'll have a coffee, and a...
a...
uhh...
uhhh
venti
no sug
x wp
cinn
dolc
iced
xtra
cup
spn
on
side

lost in conversation

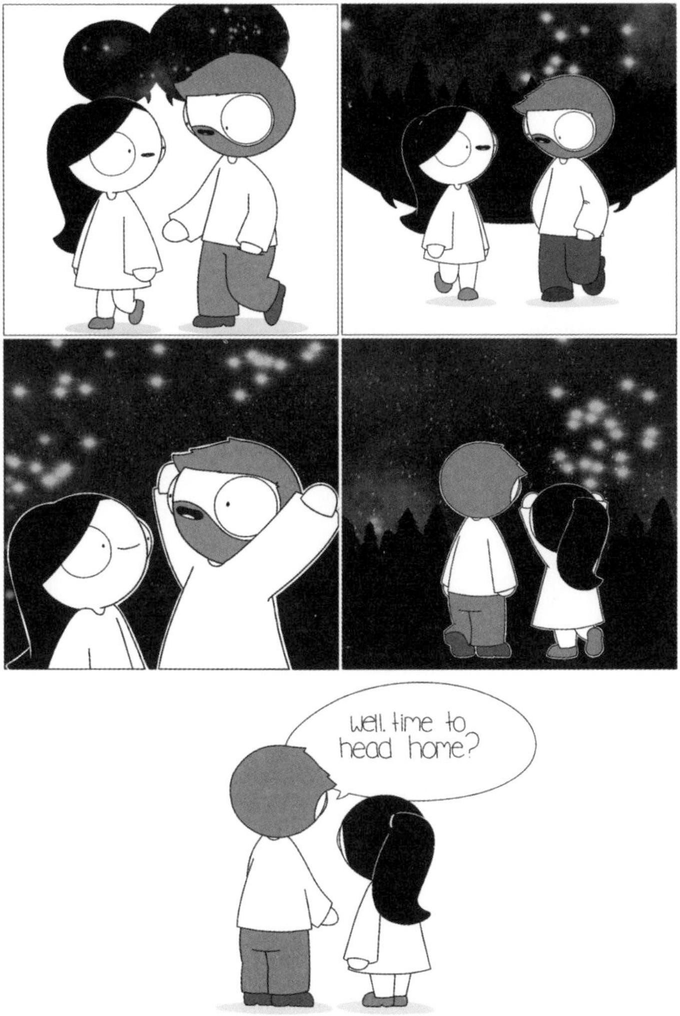
well. time to head home?

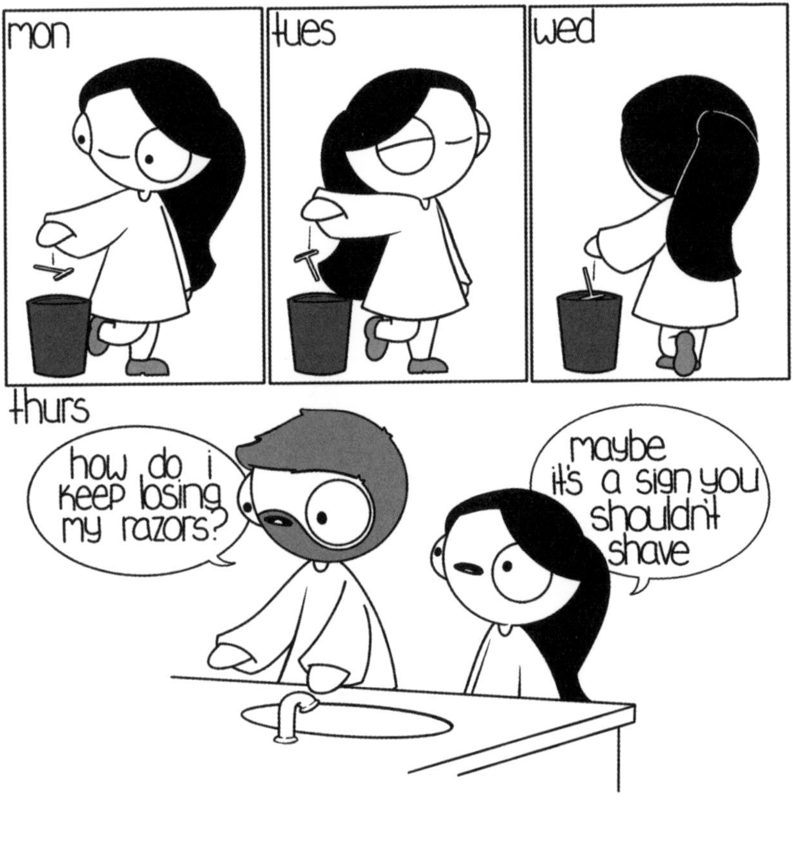
mon
tues
wed
thurs
how do i keep losing my razors?
maybe it's a sign you shouldn't shave

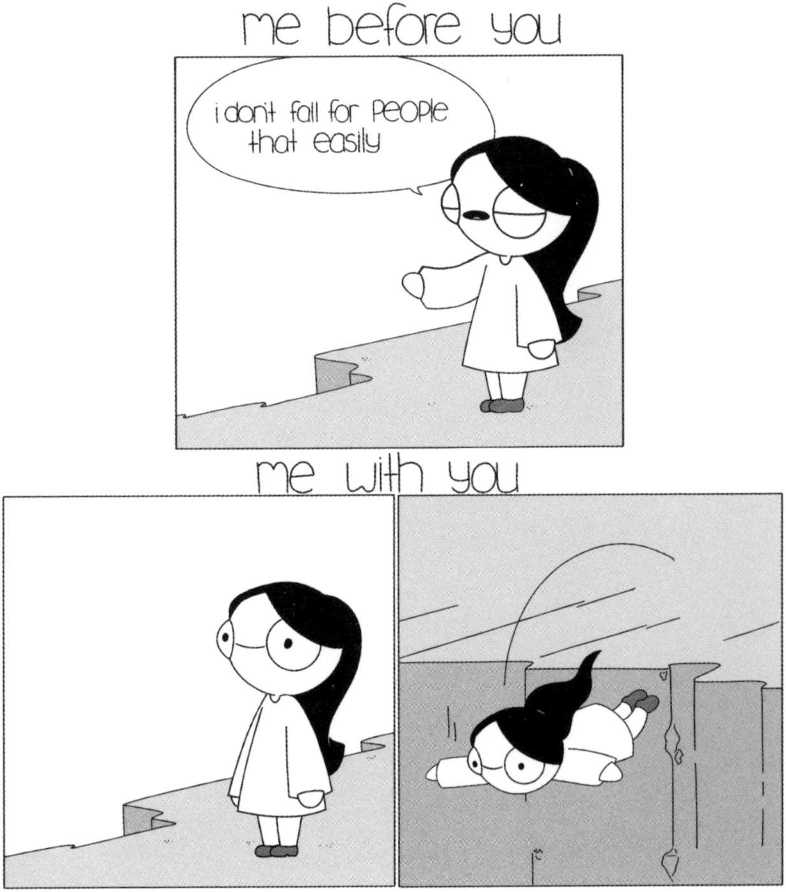
me before you
i don't fall for people
that easily
me with you

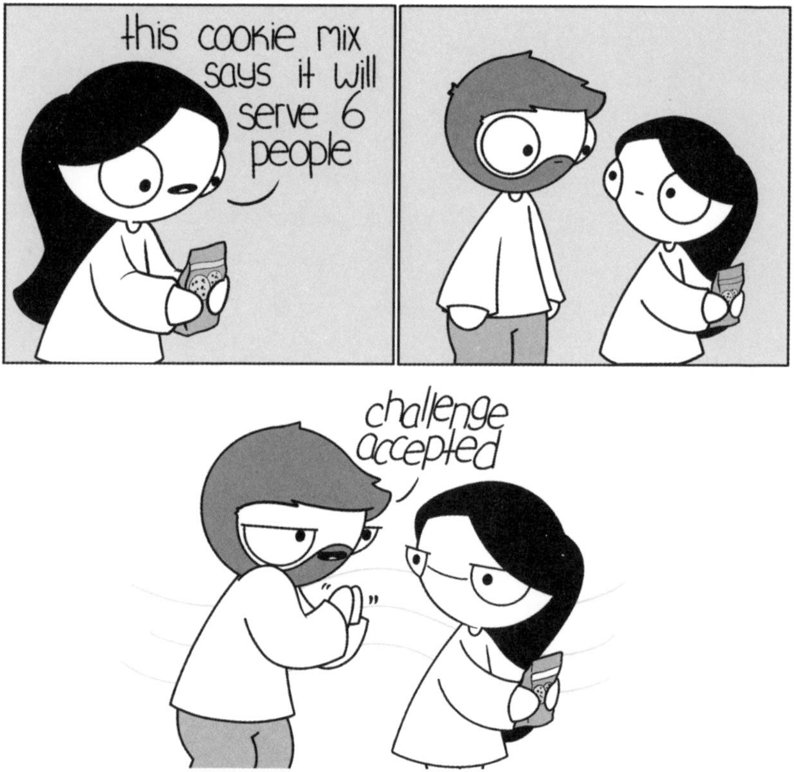
this cookie mix says it will serve 6 people
challenge accepted

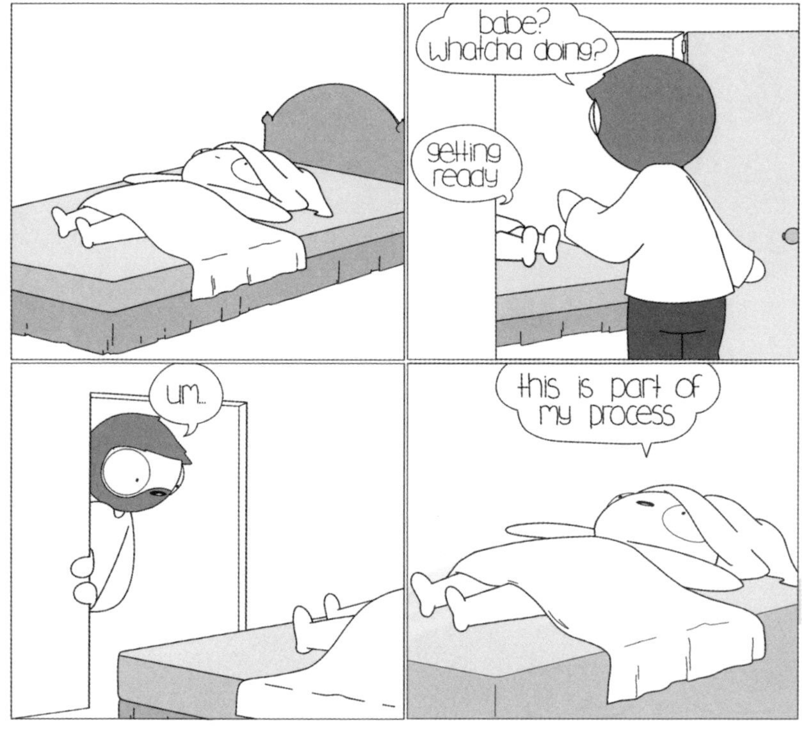
babe?
whatcha doing?
getting ready
um...
this is part of
my process

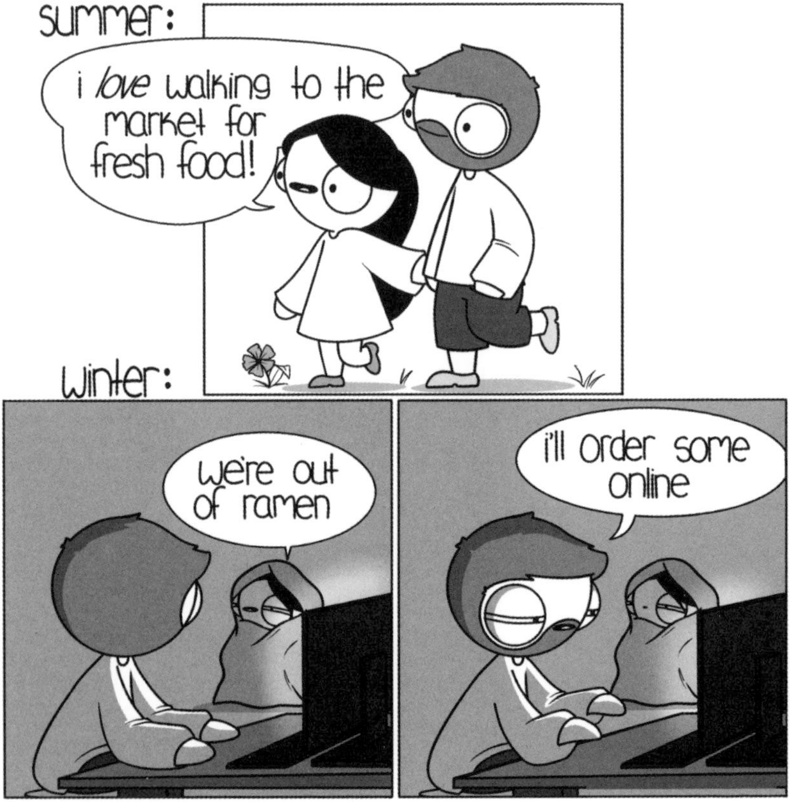
summer:
i *love* walking to the market for fresh food!
winter:
we're out of ramen
i'll order some online

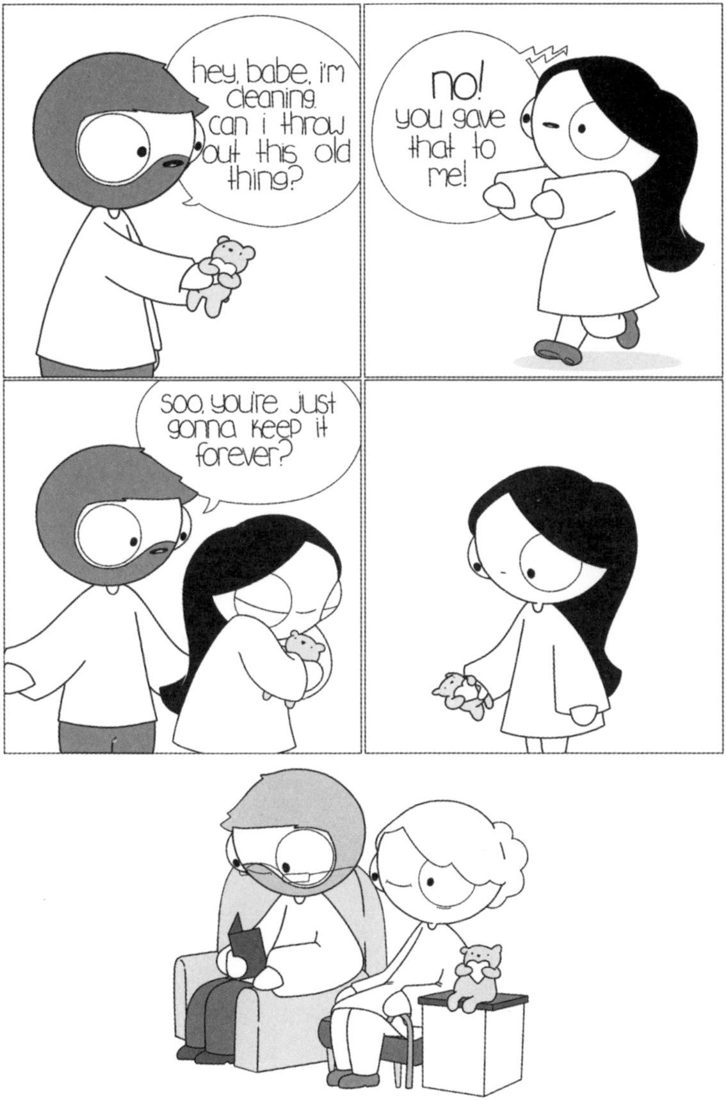
hey, babe, i'm cleaning. can i throw out this old thing?
no! you gave that to me!
soo, you're just gonna keep it forever?

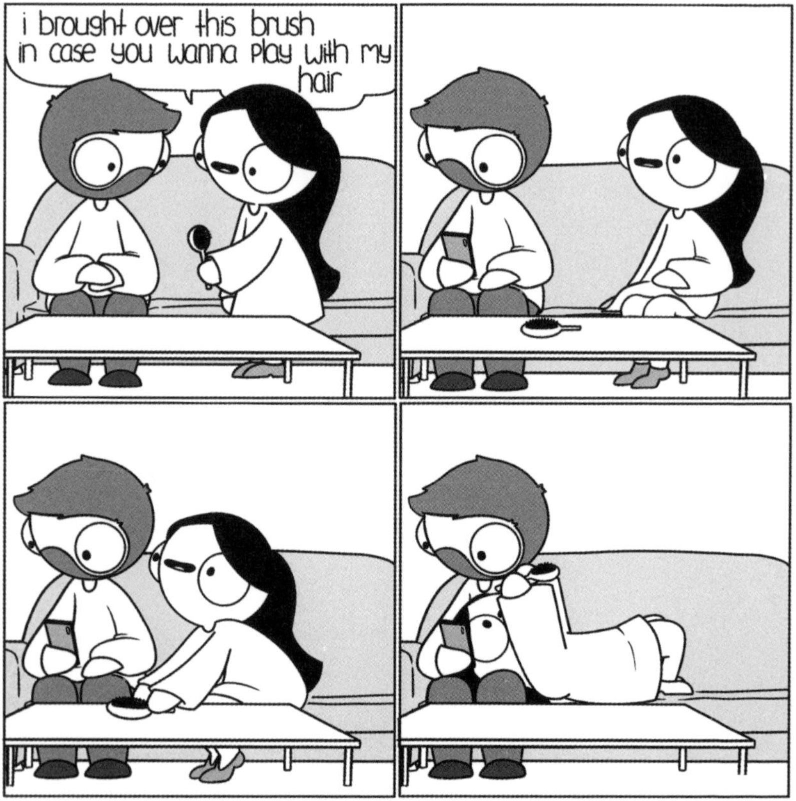
i brought over this brush in case you wanna play with my hair

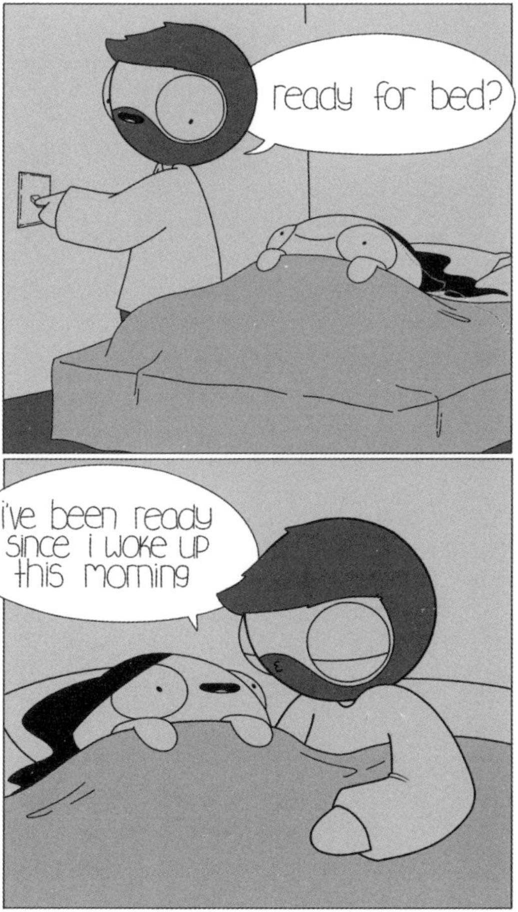
ready for bed?
i've been ready since i woke up this morning

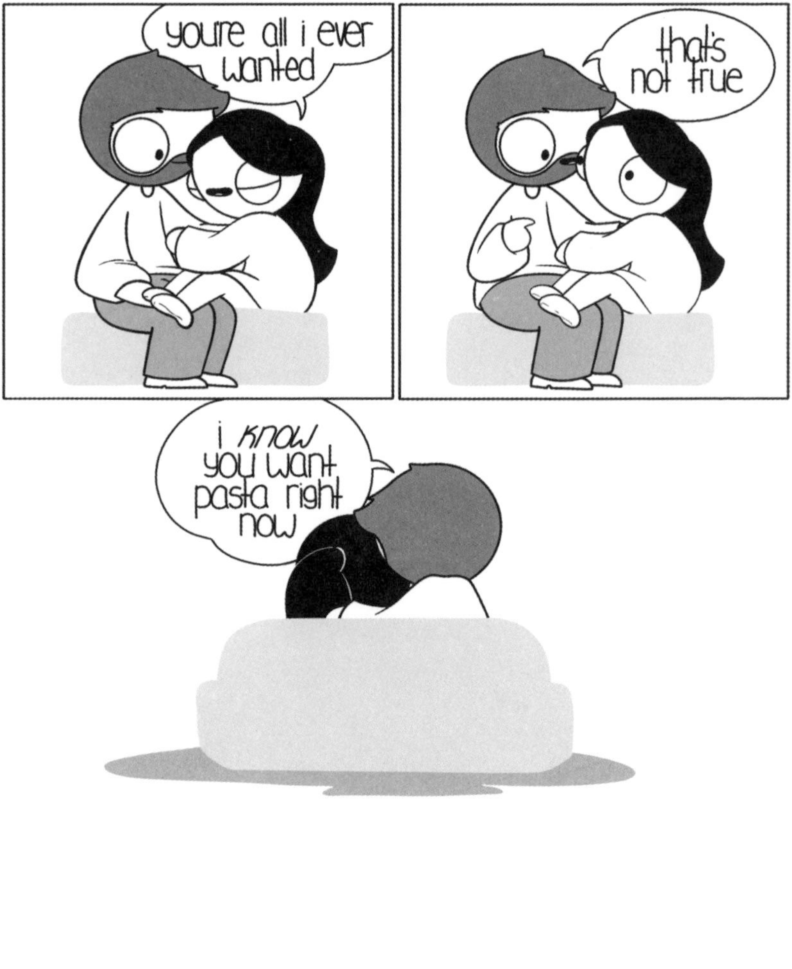
you're all i ever wanted
that's not true
i *know* you want pasta right now

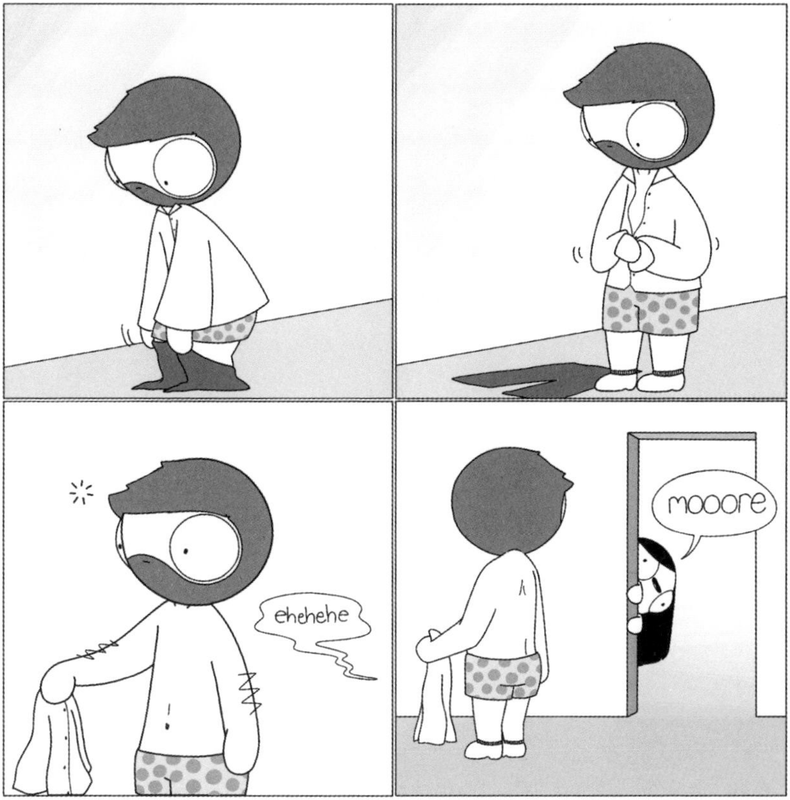
ehehehe
mooore

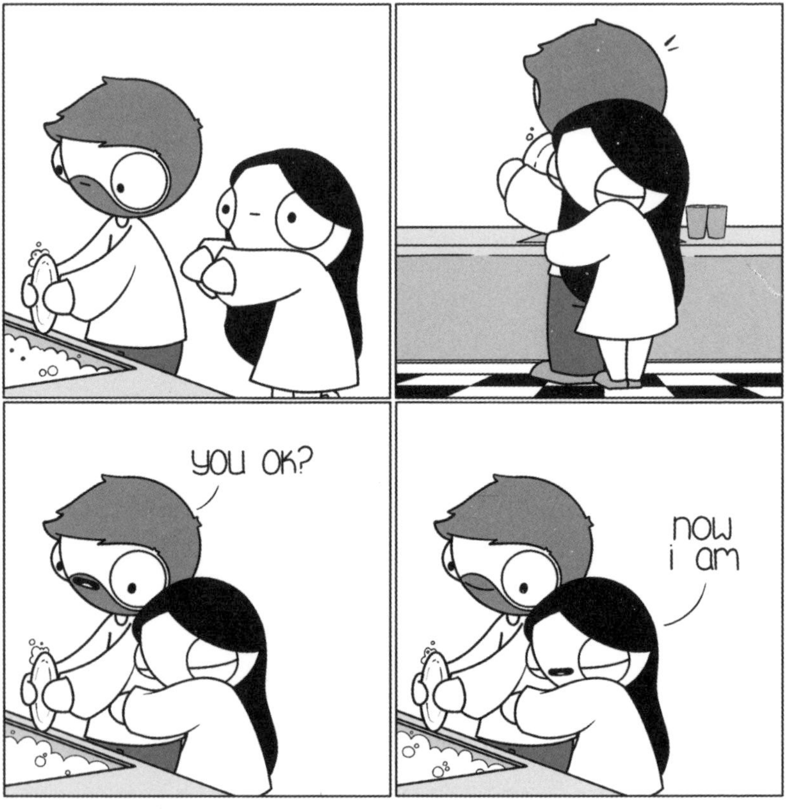
you ok?
now
i am

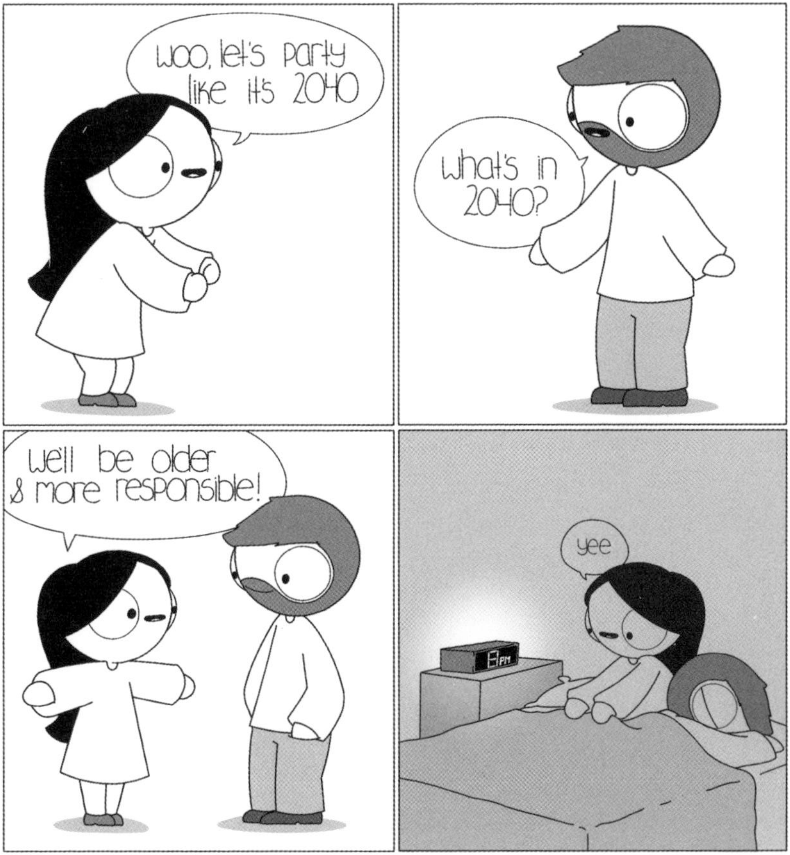
woo, let's party like it's 2040
What's in 2040?
We'll be older & more responsible!
yee
8PM

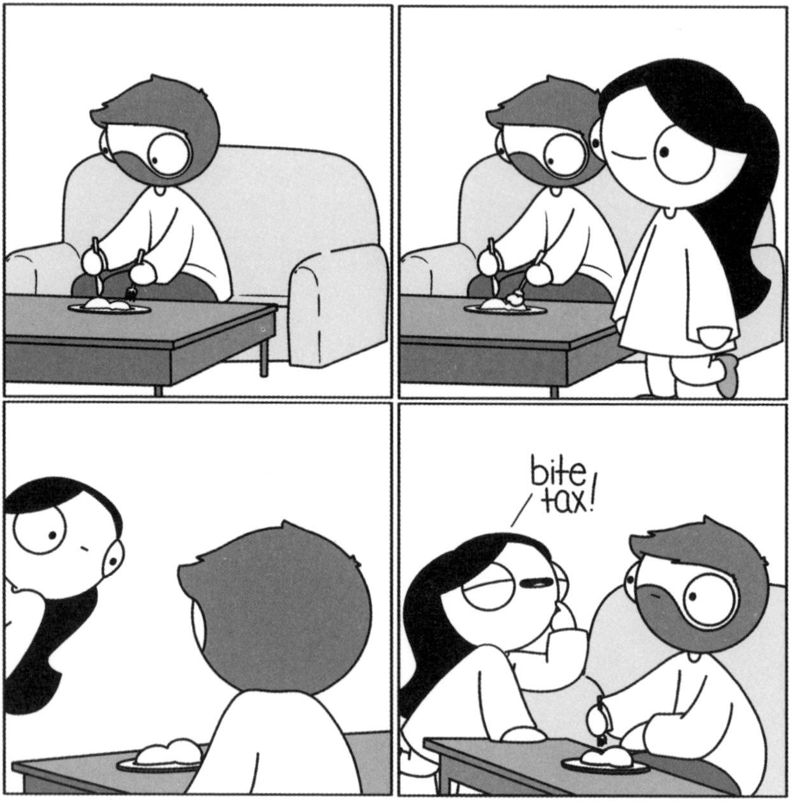
bite tax!

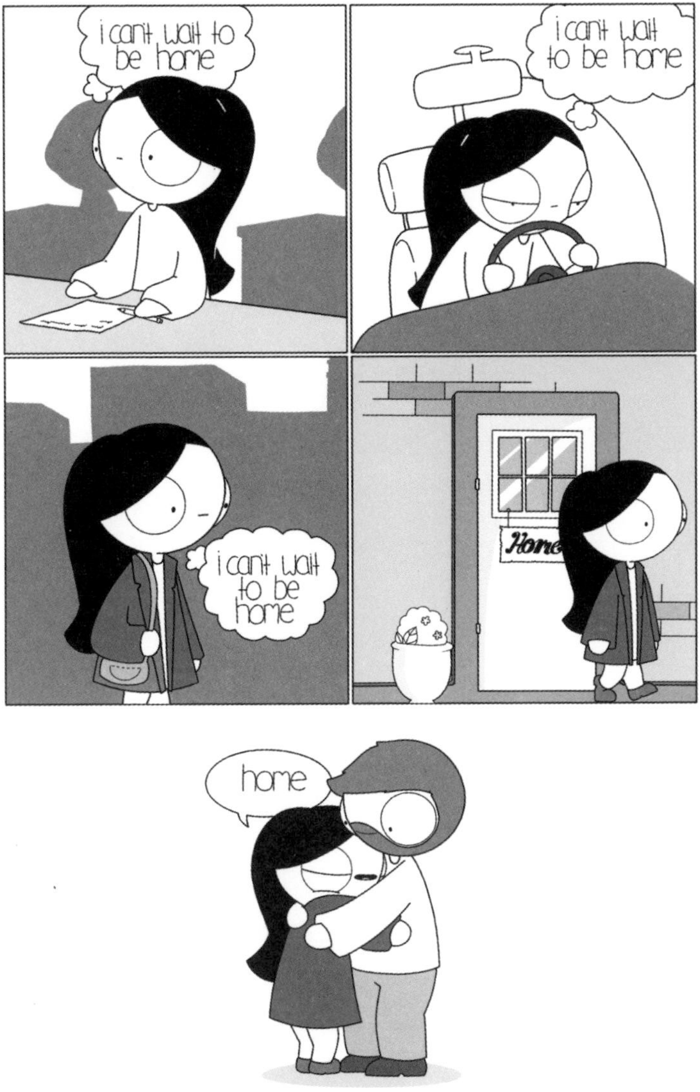
i can't wait to be home
i can't wait to be home
i can't wait to be home
Home
home

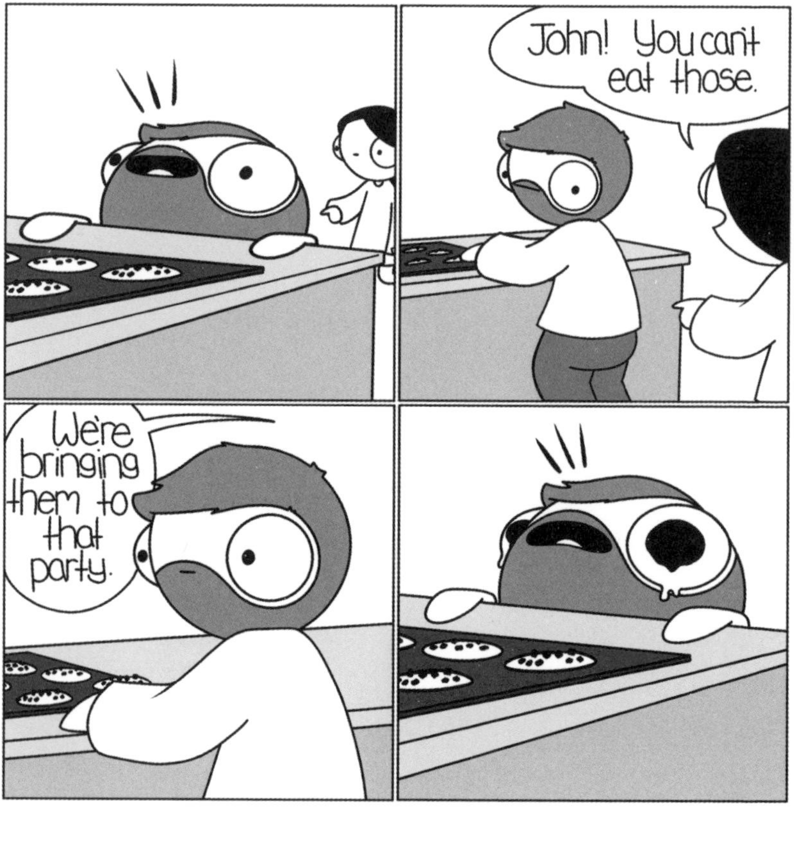
John! You can't eat those.
We're bringing them to that party.

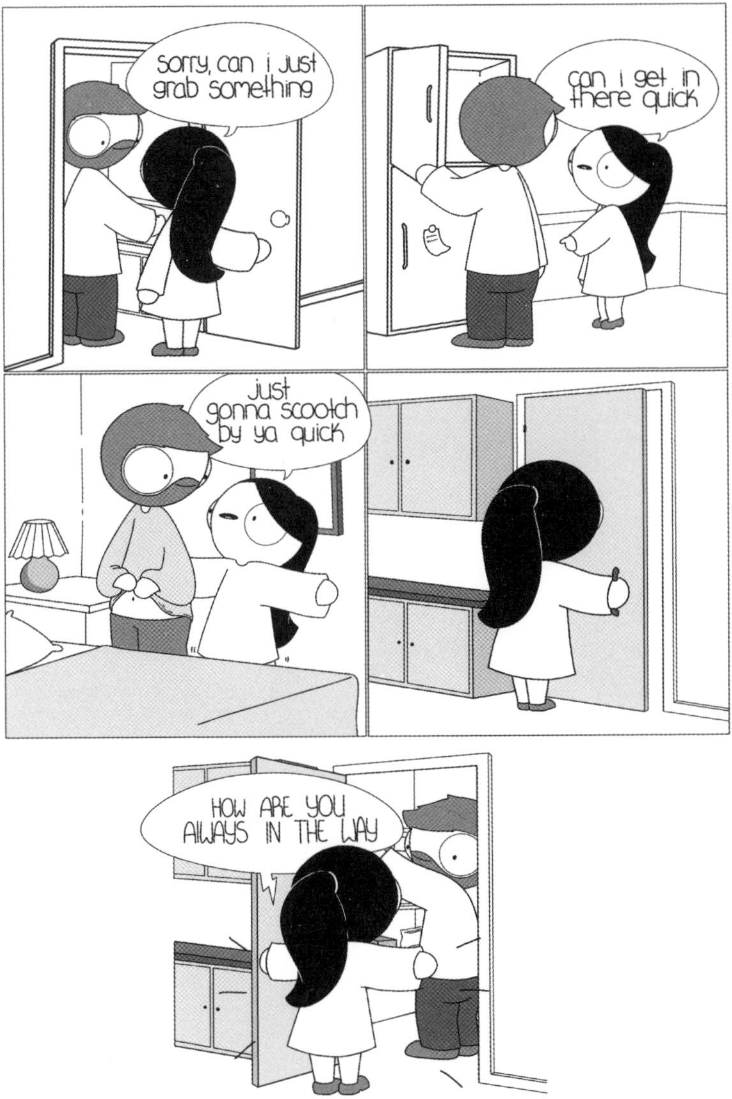
sorry, can i just grab something
can i get in there quick
just gonna scootch by ya quick
HOW ARE YOU ALWAYS IN THE WAY

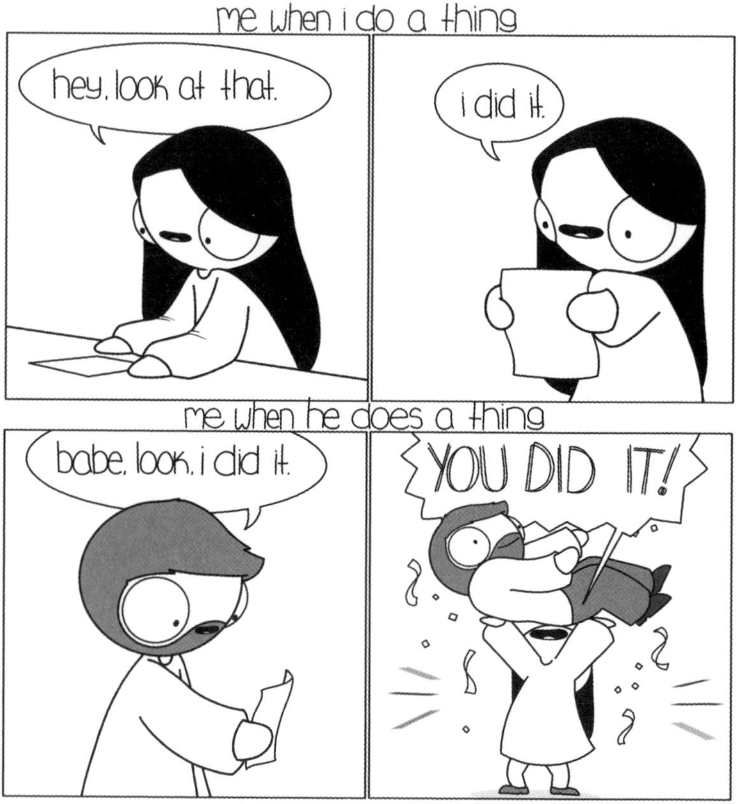
me when i do a thing
hey, look at that.
i did it.
me when he does a thing
babe, look, i did it.
YOU DID IT!

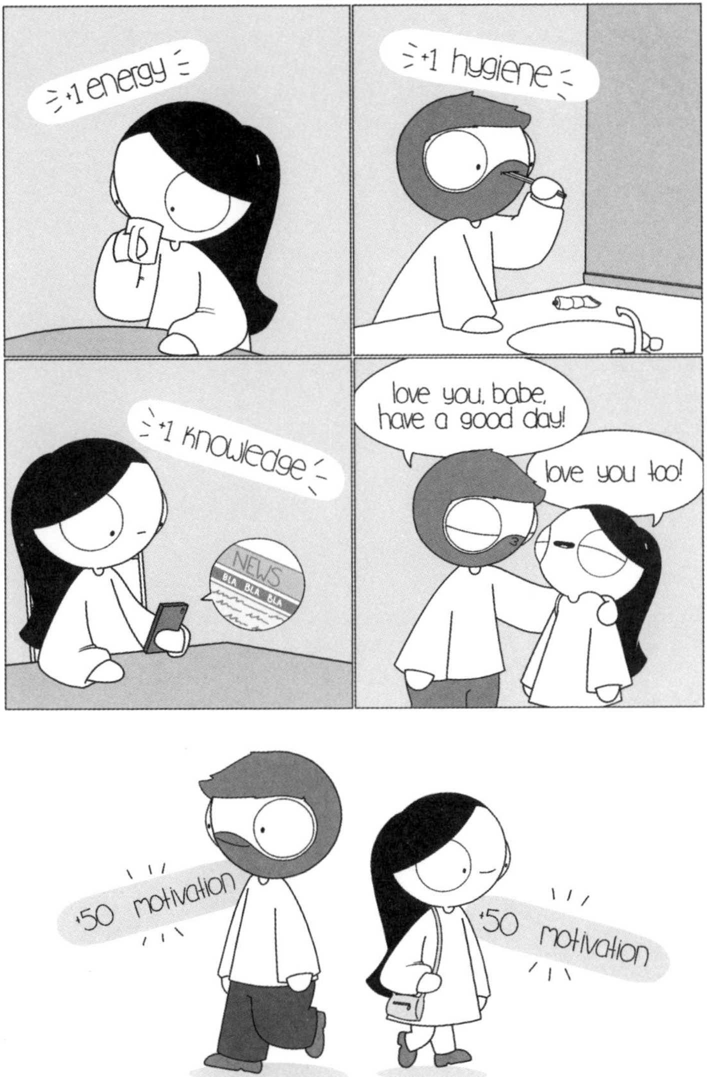
+1 energy
+1 hygiene
+1 knowledge
NEWS
BLA BLA BLA
love you, babe, have a good day!
love you too!
+50 motivation
+50 motivation

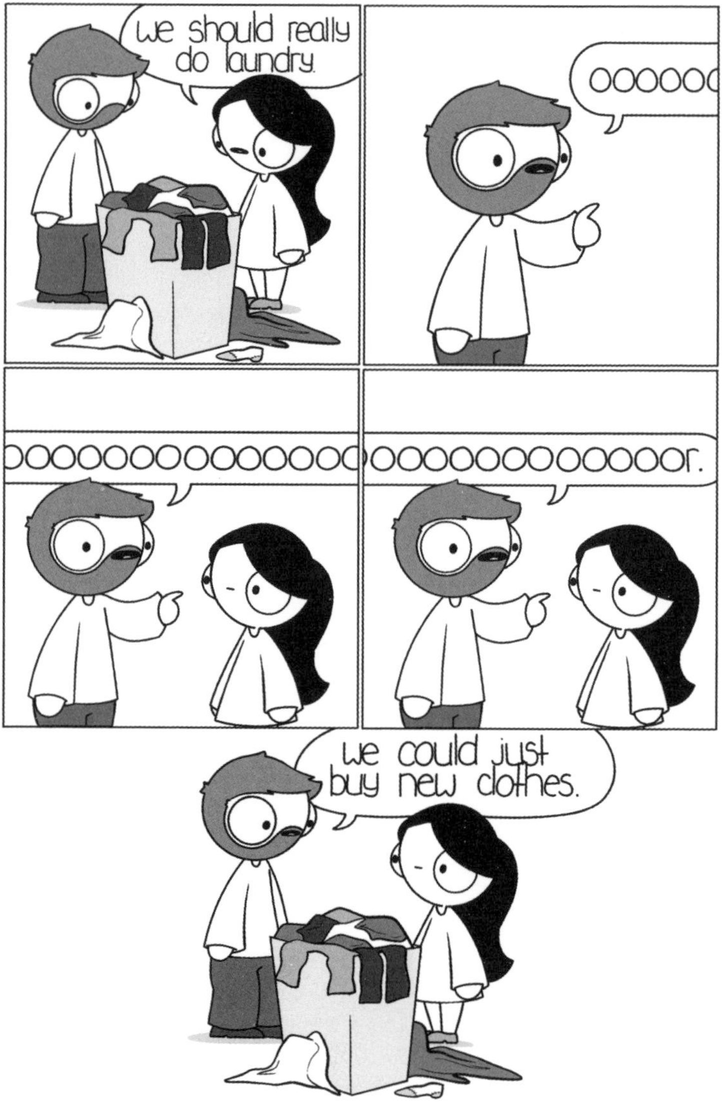
we should really do laundry.
ooooo
ooooooooooooooo
oooooooooooooor.
we could just buy new clothes.

Reasons why i'm smiling at my phone

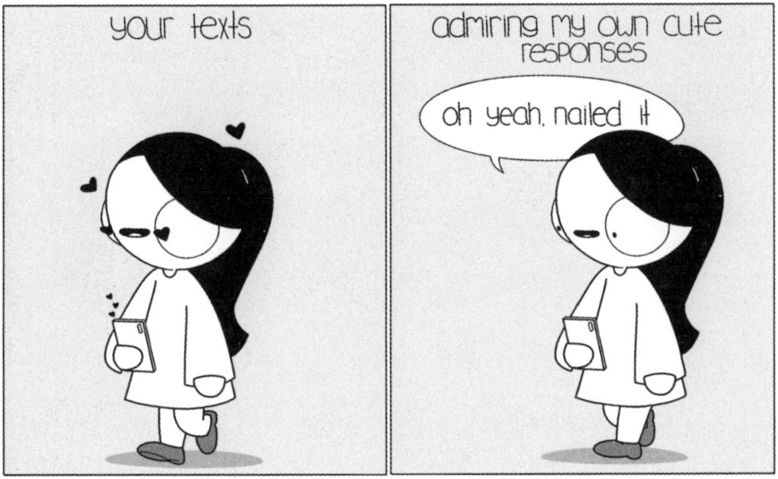
your texts
admiring my own cute responses
oh yeah, nailed it

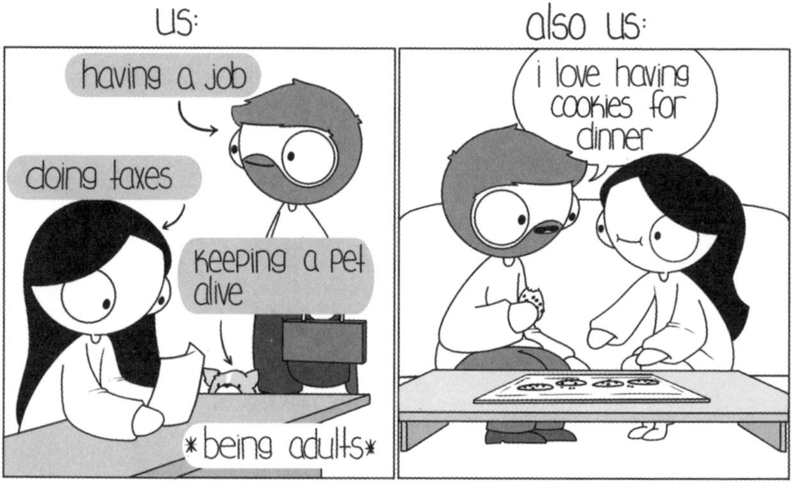
us:
having a job
doing taxes
keeping a pet alive
being adults
also us:
i love having cookies for dinner

reason #174 to love fall

wearing enough layers to hide your food babies

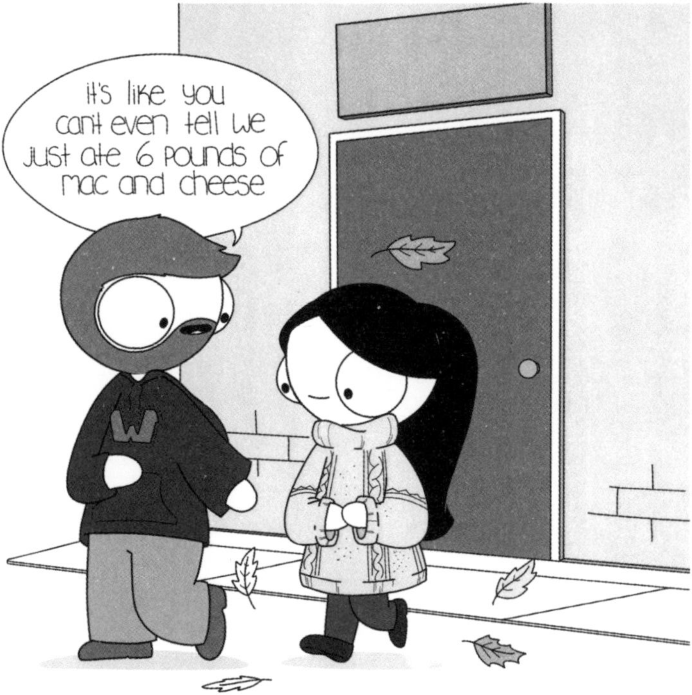
it's like you can't even tell we just ate 6 pounds of mac and cheese

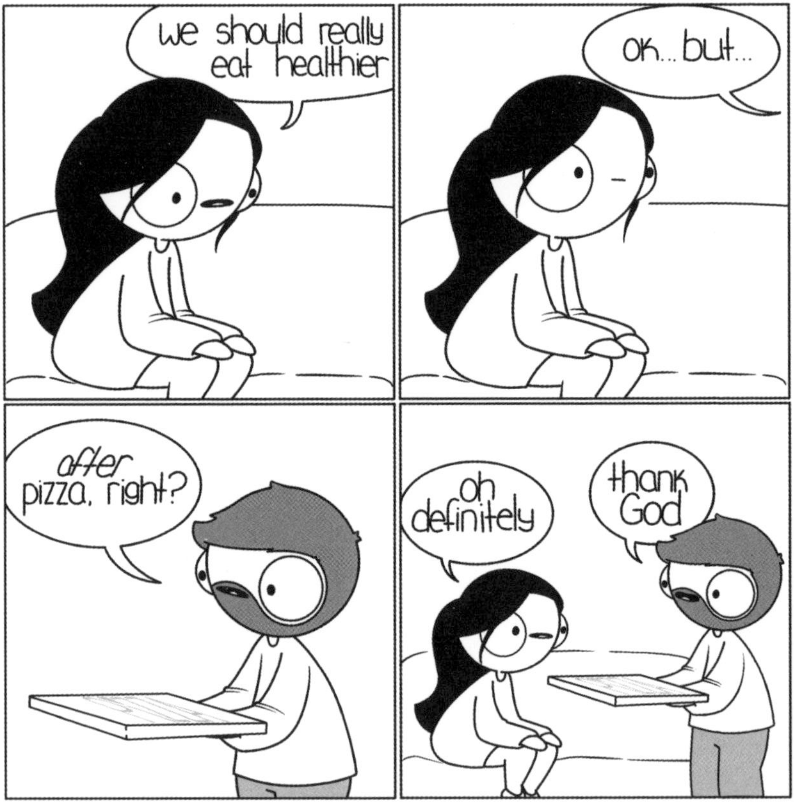
we should really eat healthier
ok... but...
after pizza, right?
oh definitely
thank God

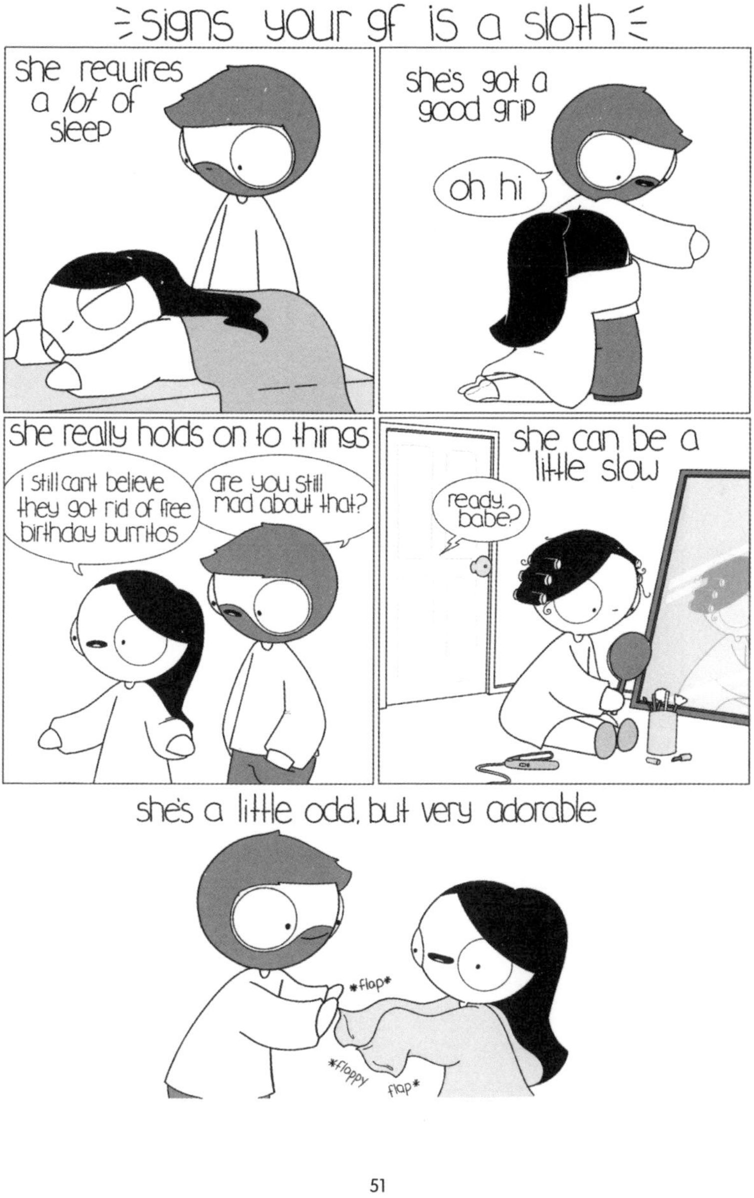
signs your gf is a sloth
she requires a lot of sleep
she's got a good grip
oh hi
she really holds on to things
i still cant believe they got rid of free birthday burritos
are you still mad about that?
she can be a little slow
ready, babe?
she's a little odd, but very adorable
flap
floppy flap

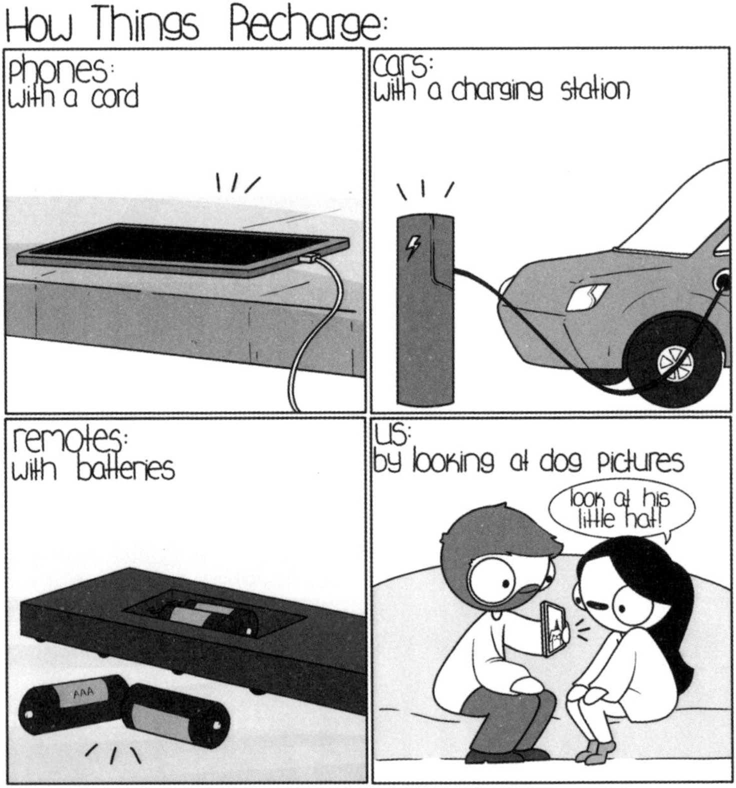
How Things Recharge:
phones:
with a cord
cars:
with a charging station
remotes:
with batteries
AAA
us:
by looking at dog pictures
look at his little hat!

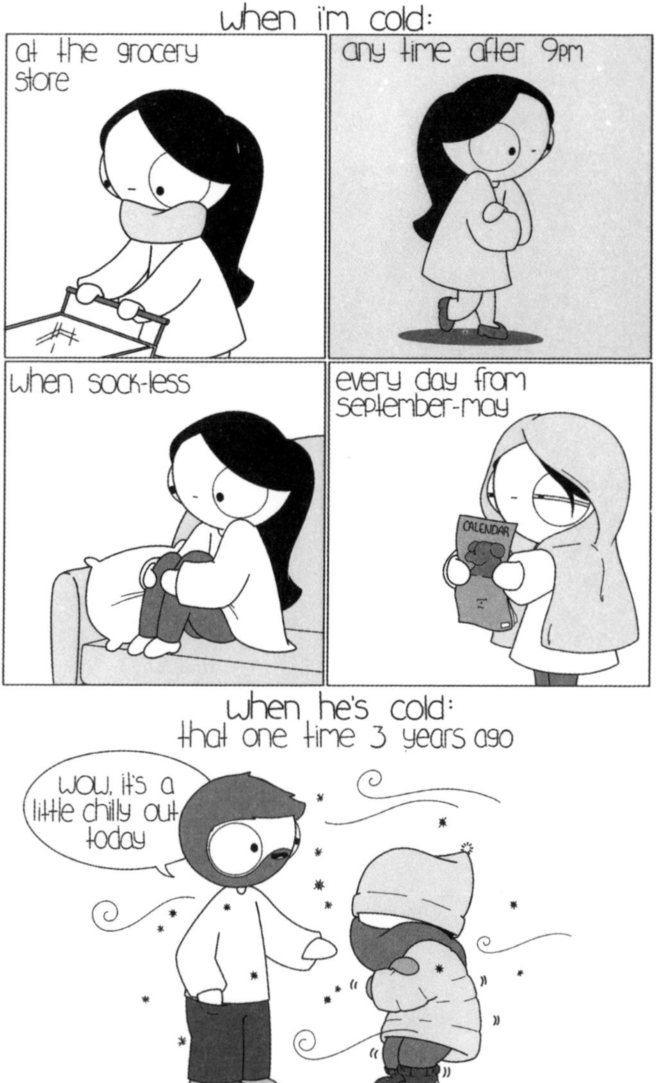
when i'm cold:
at the grocery store
any time after 9pm
when sock-less
every day from september-may
CALENDAR
when he's cold:
that one time 3 years ago
wow, it's a little chilly out today

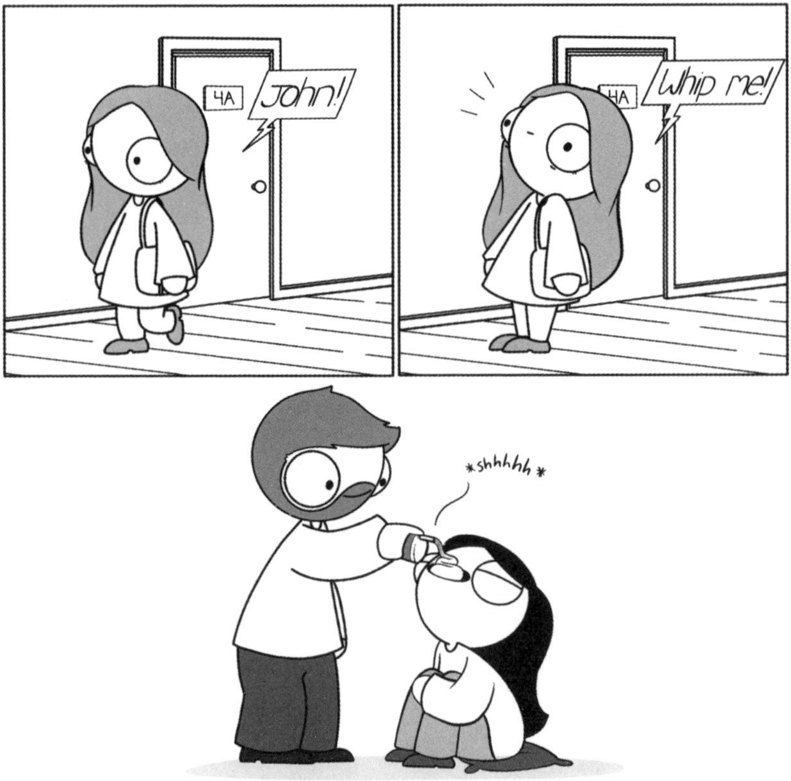
4A
John!
4A
Whip me!
shhhhh

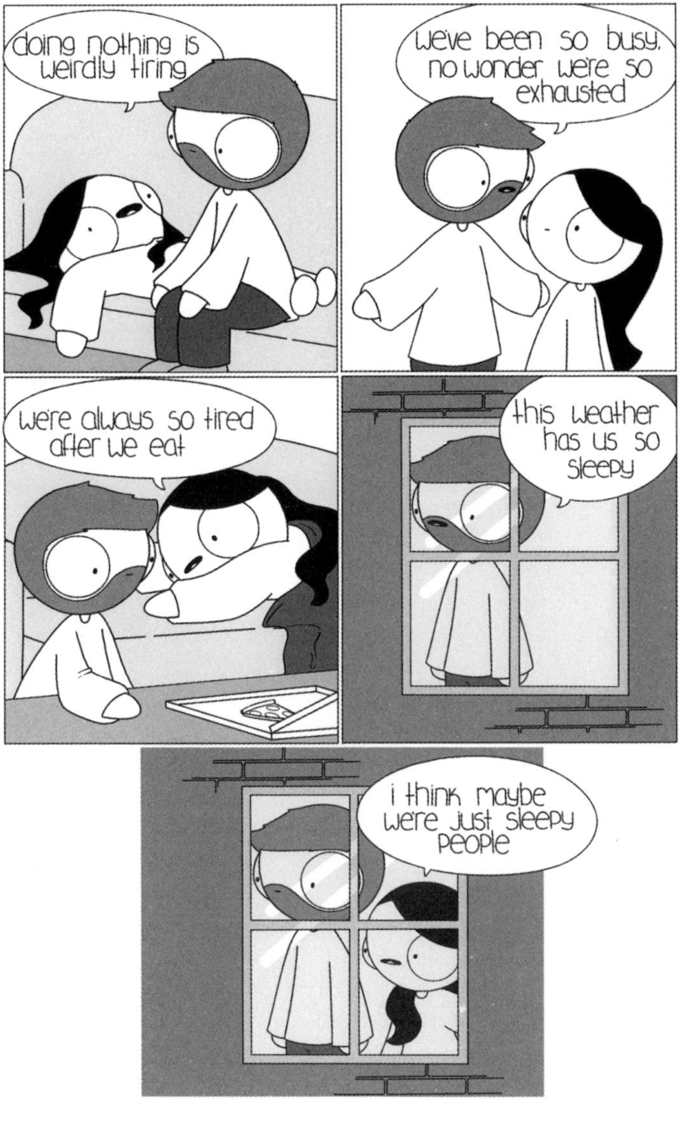
doing nothing is weirdly tiring
we've been so busy, no wonder we're so exhausted
we're always so tired after we eat
this weather has us so sleepy
i think maybe we're just sleepy people

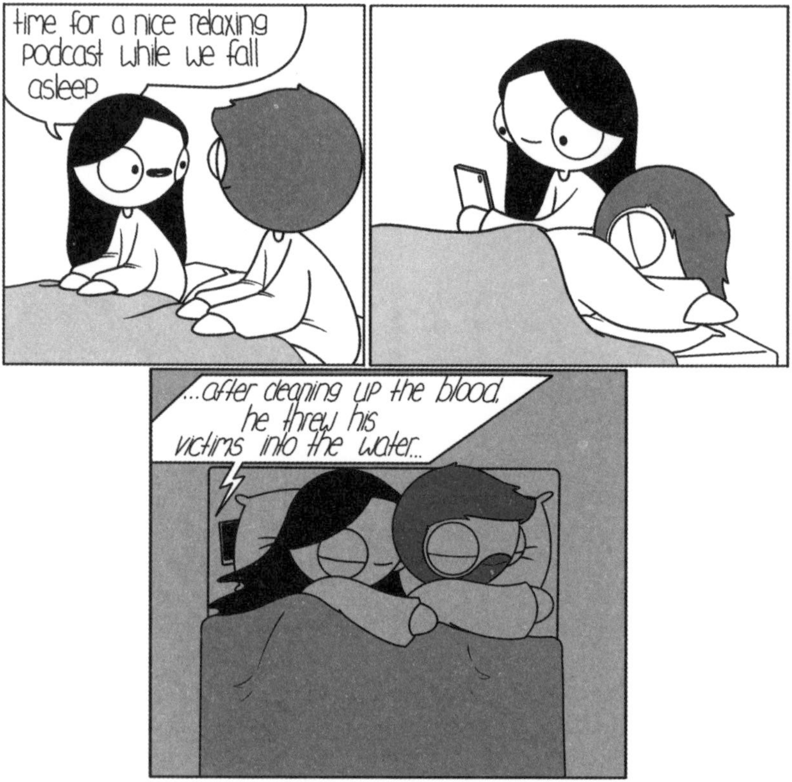
time for a nice relaxing podcast while we fall asleep
...after cleaning up the blood, he threw his victims into the water...

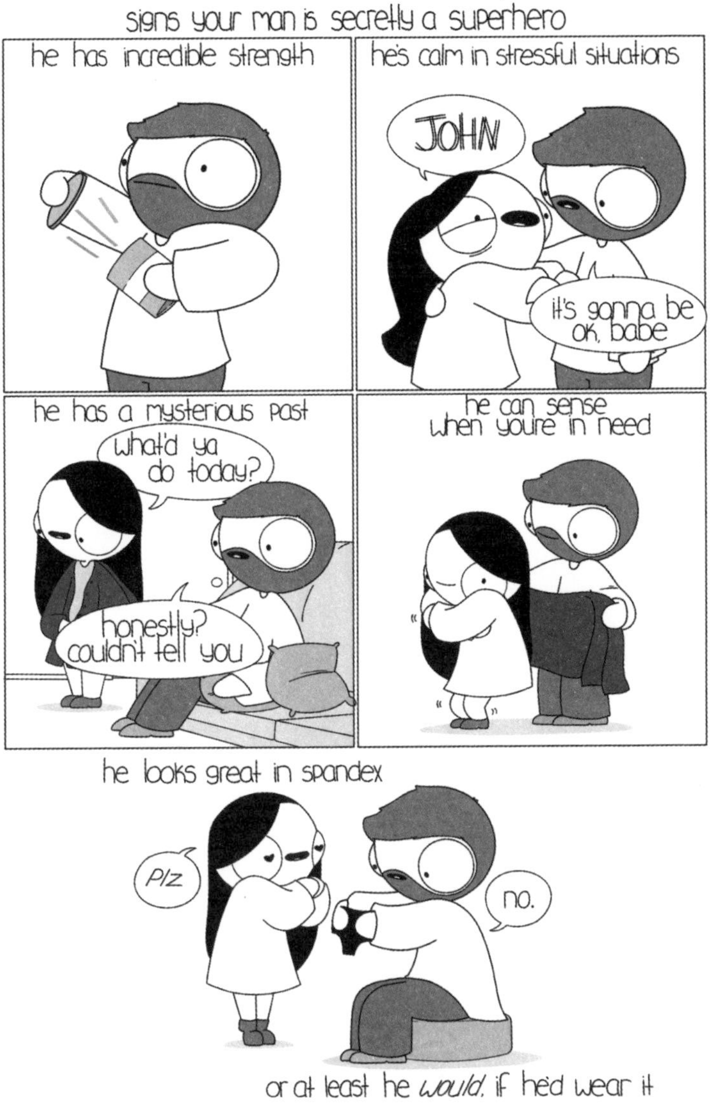
signs your man is secretly a superhero
he has incredible strength
he's calm in stressful situations
JOHN
it's gonna be ok, babe
he has a mysterious past
what'd ya do today?
honestly? couldn't tell you
he can sense when you're in need
he looks great in spandex
Plz
no.
or at least he *would*, if he'd wear it

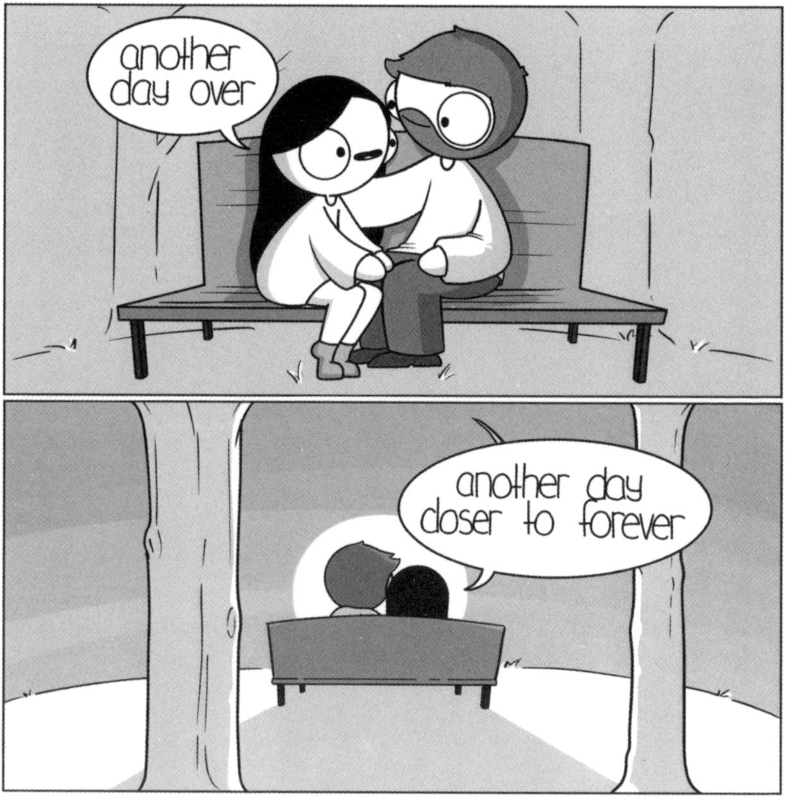
another day over
another day closer to forever

when babe's upset

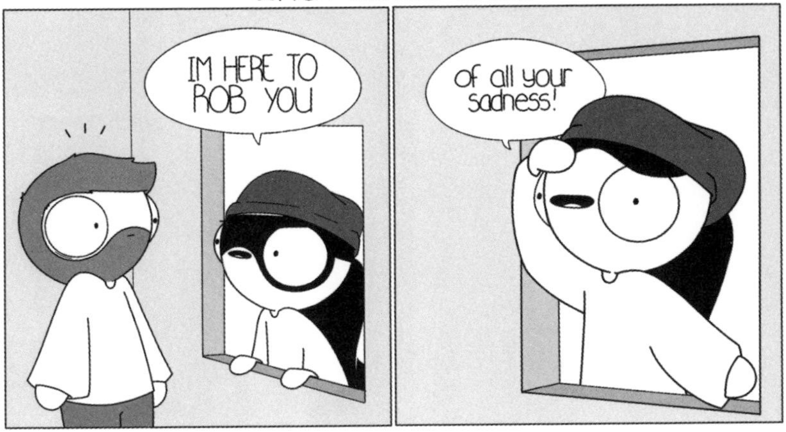
IM HERE TO ROB YOU
of all your sadness!

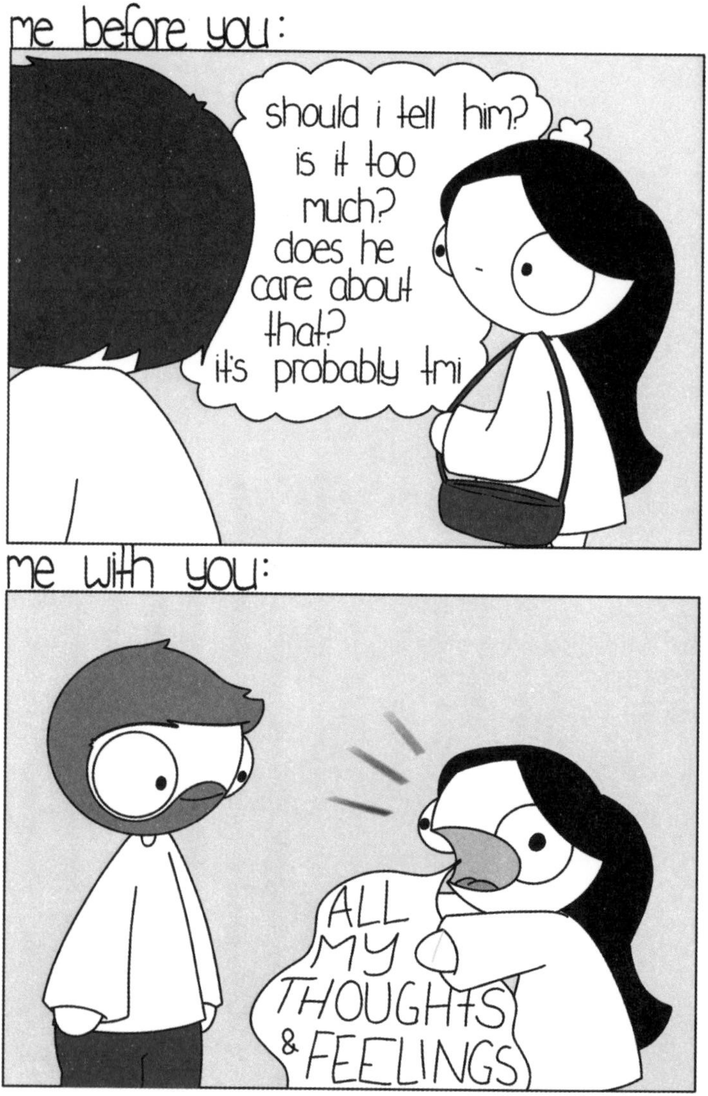
me before you:
should i tell him? is it too much? does he care about that? it's probably tmi
me with you:
ALL MY THOUGHTS & FEELINGS

reasons why i might be stressed

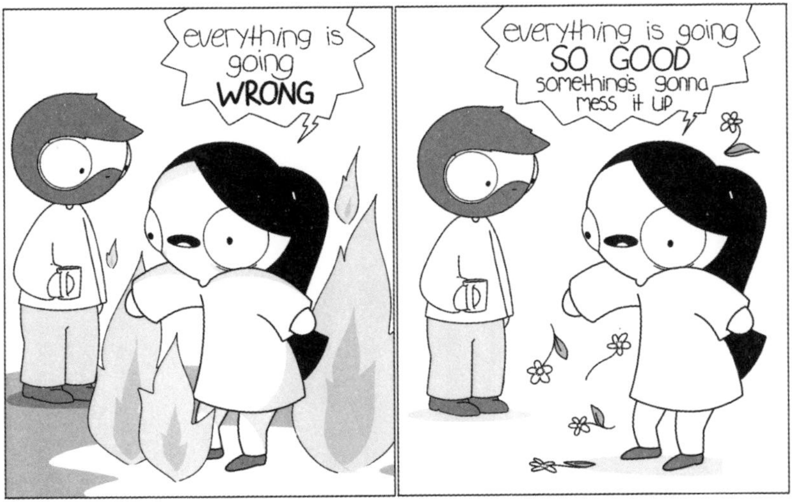
everything is going WRONG
everything is going SO GOOD something's gonna mess it up

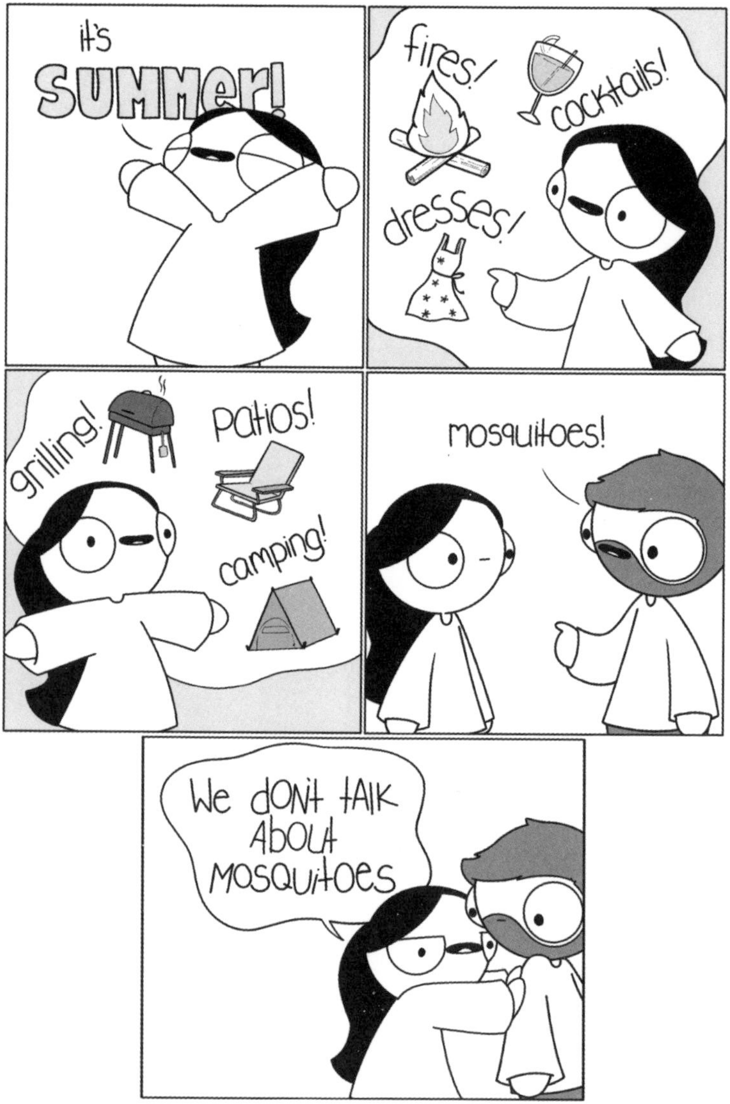
it's
SUMMER!
fires!
cocktails!
dresses!
grilling!
Patios!
camping!
mosquitoes!
We don't talk
About
Mosquitoes

telling a story

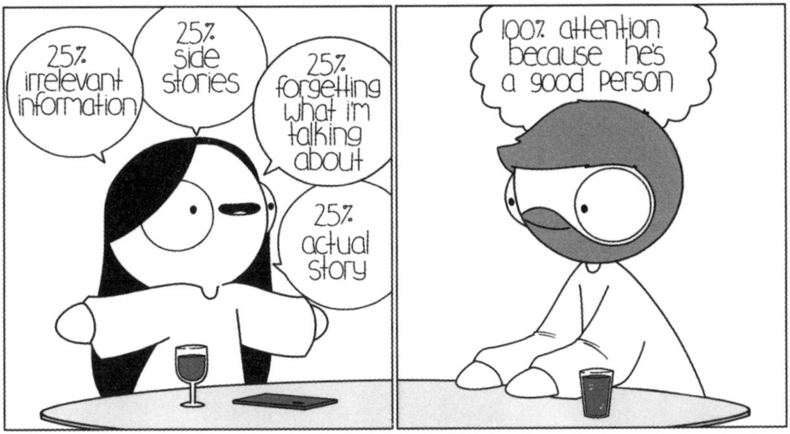
25% irrelevant information
25% side stories
25% forgetting what i'm talking about
25% actual story
100% attention because he's a good person

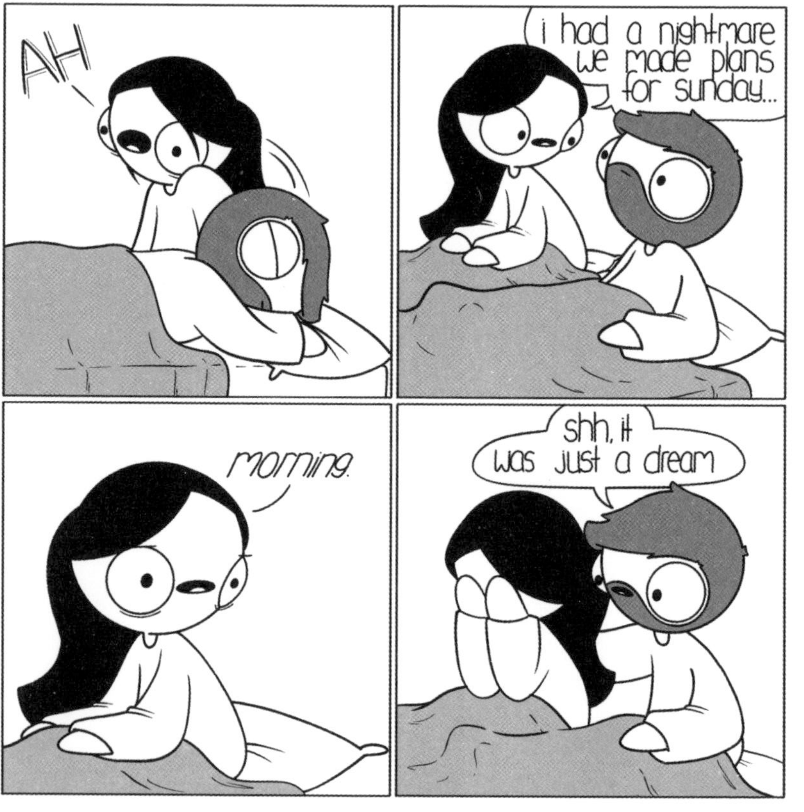
AH
i had a nightmare we made plans for sunday...
morning.
shh, it was just a dream

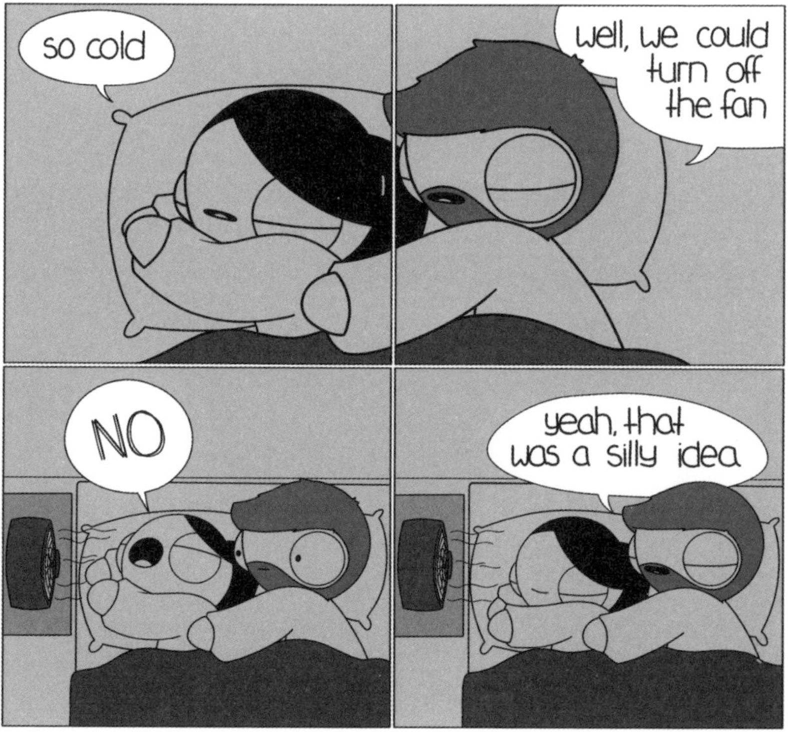
so cold
well, we could turn off the fan
NO
yeah, that was a silly idea

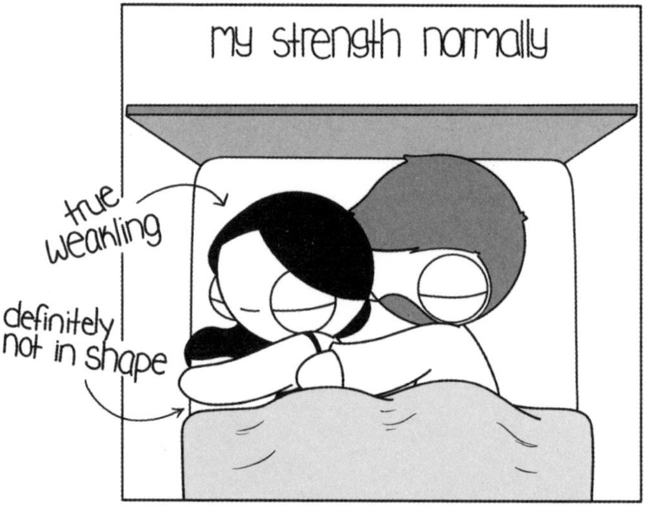
my strength normally
true weakling
definitely not in shape

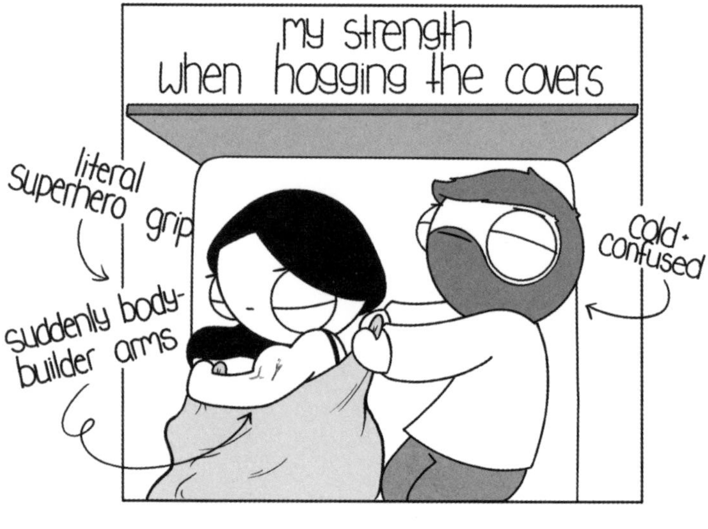
my strength when hogging the covers
literal superhero grip
suddenly body-builder arms
cold + confused

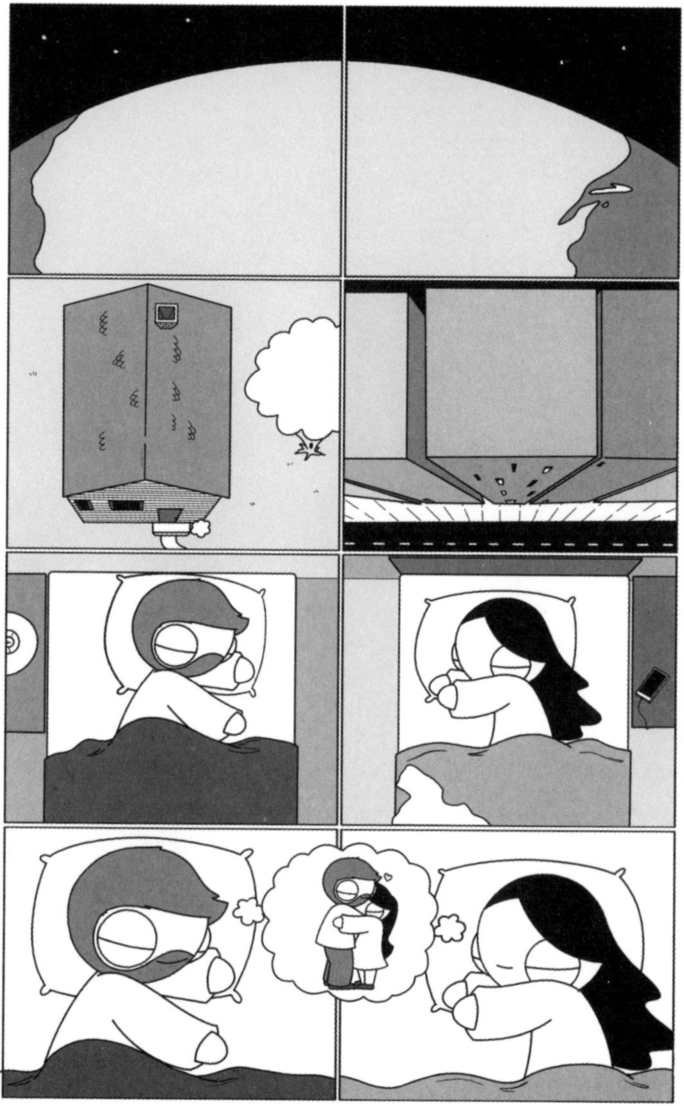

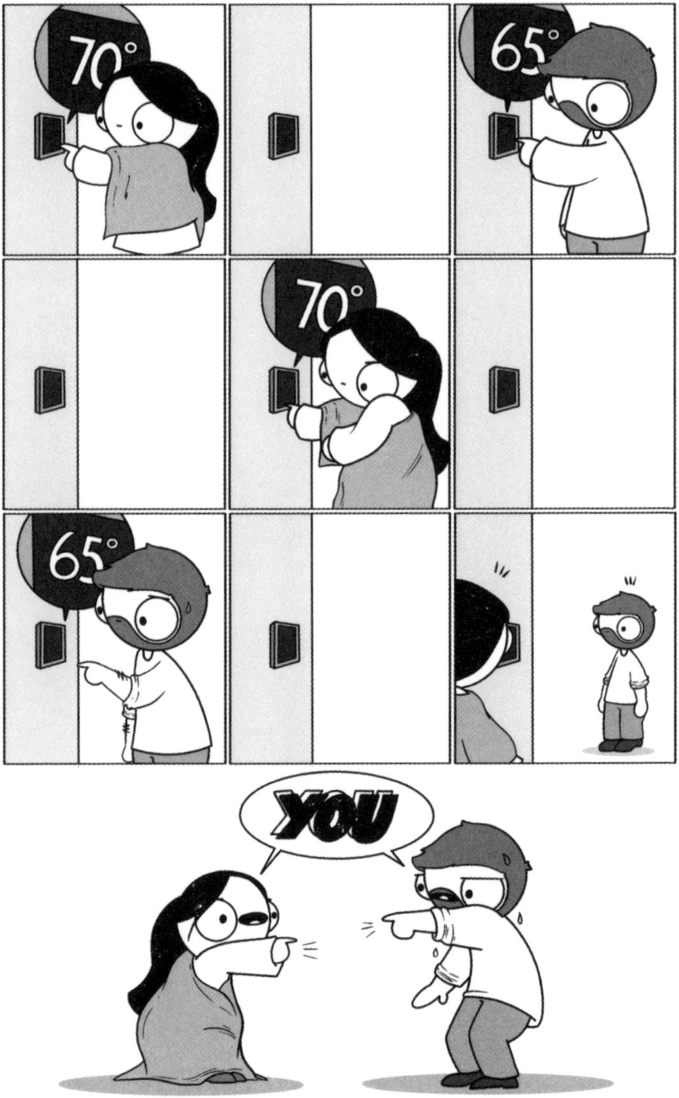
70°
65°
70°
65°
YOU

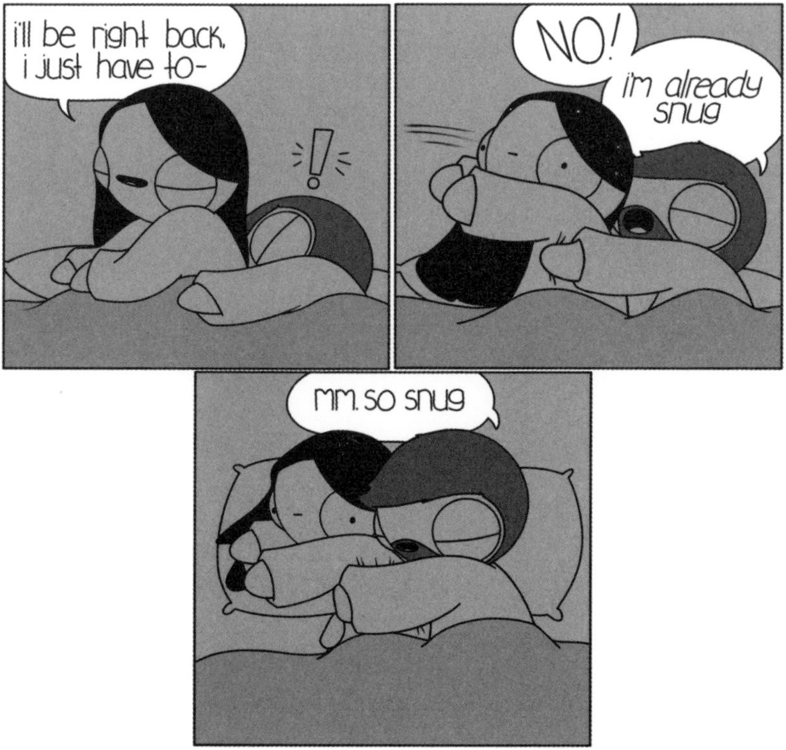
i'll be right back. i just have to-
!
NO!
i'm already snug
mm. so snug

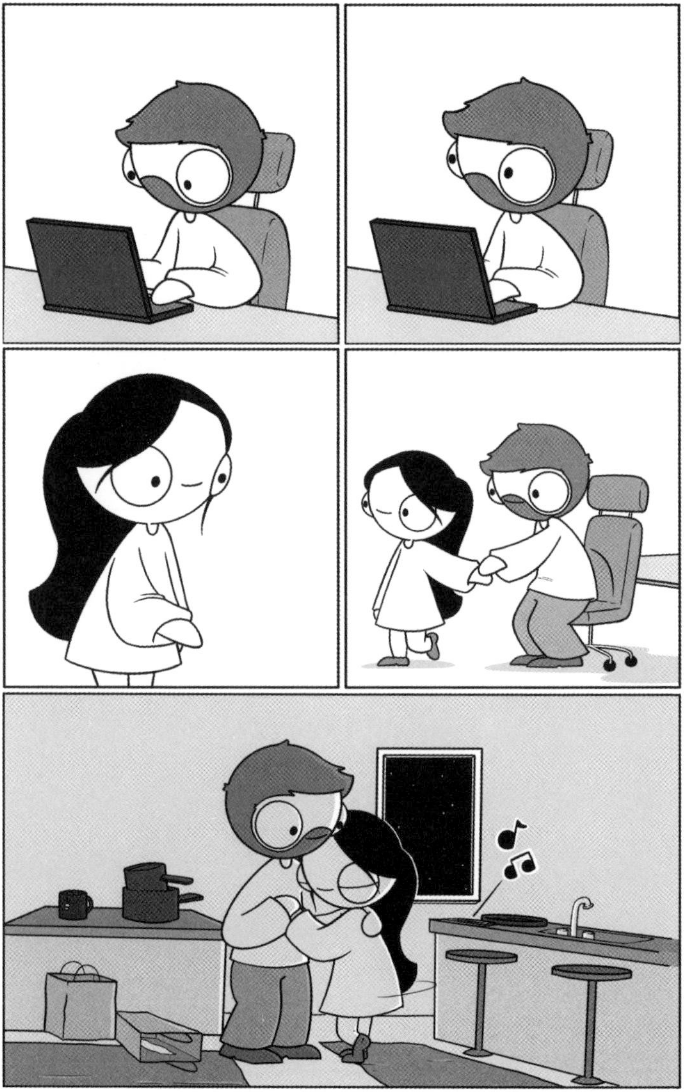

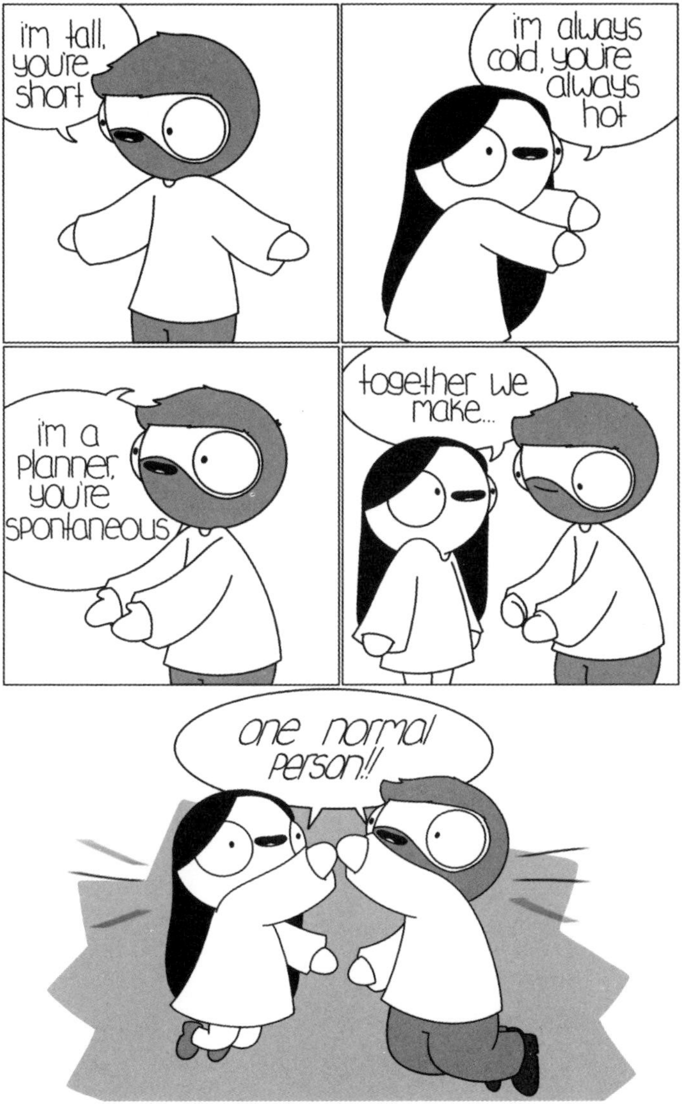
i'm tall, you're short
i'm always cold, you're always hot
i'm a planner, you're spontaneous
together we make...
one normal person!!

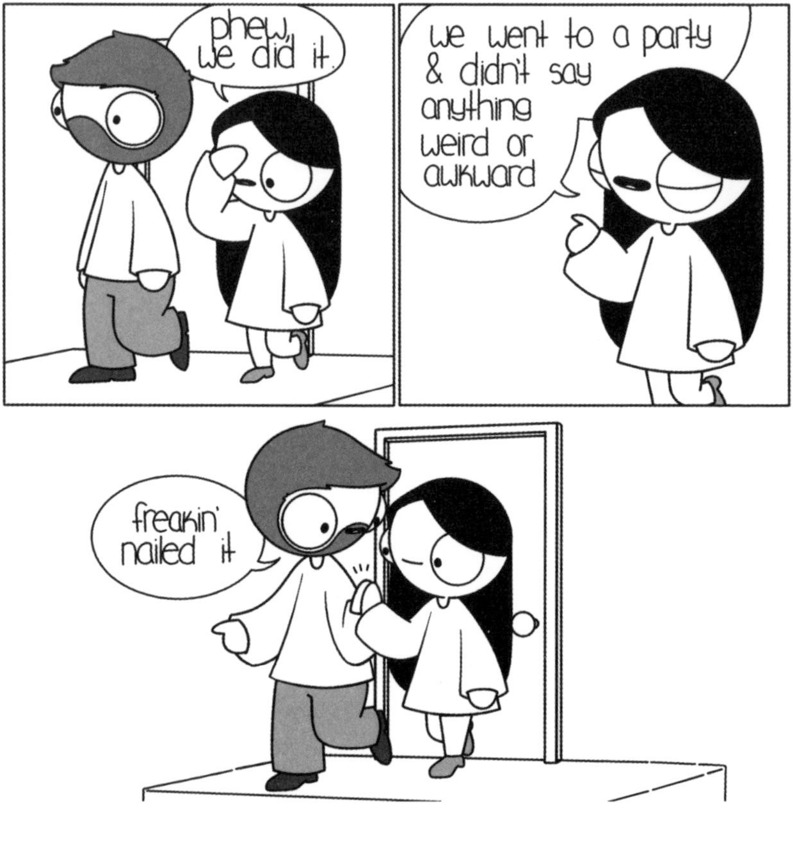
phew, we did it.
we went to a party & didn't say anything weird or awkward
freakin' nailed it

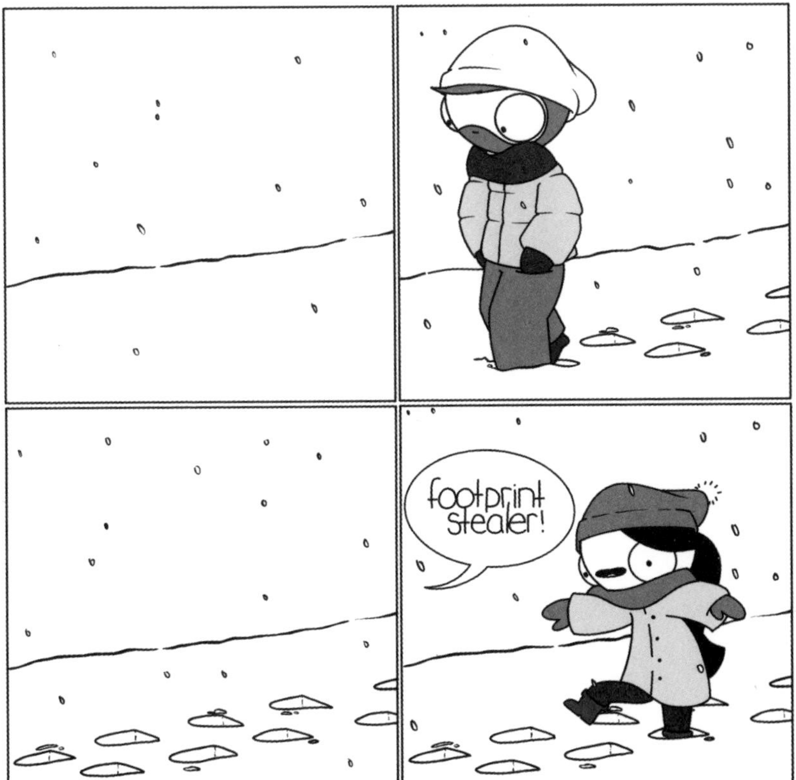
footprint stealer!

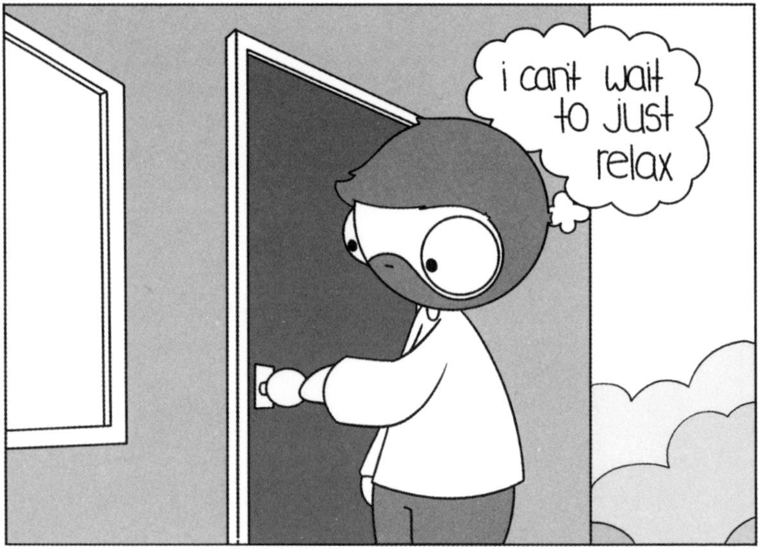
i can't wait to just relax

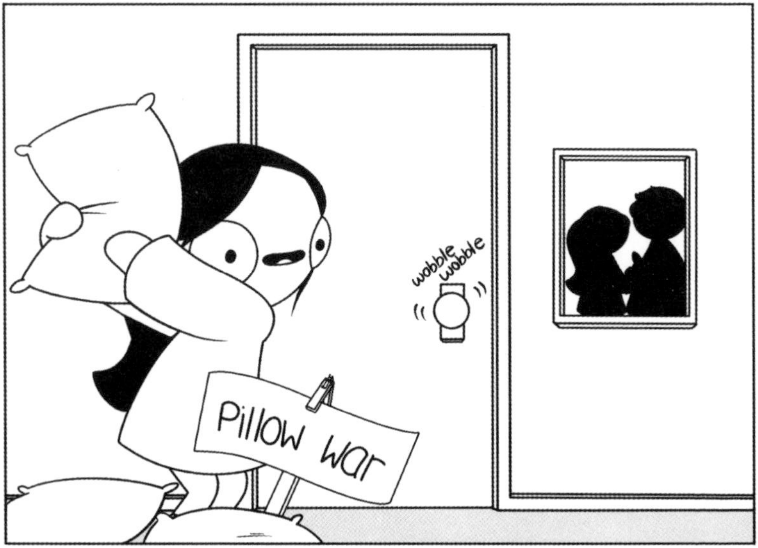
wobble wobble
Pillow war

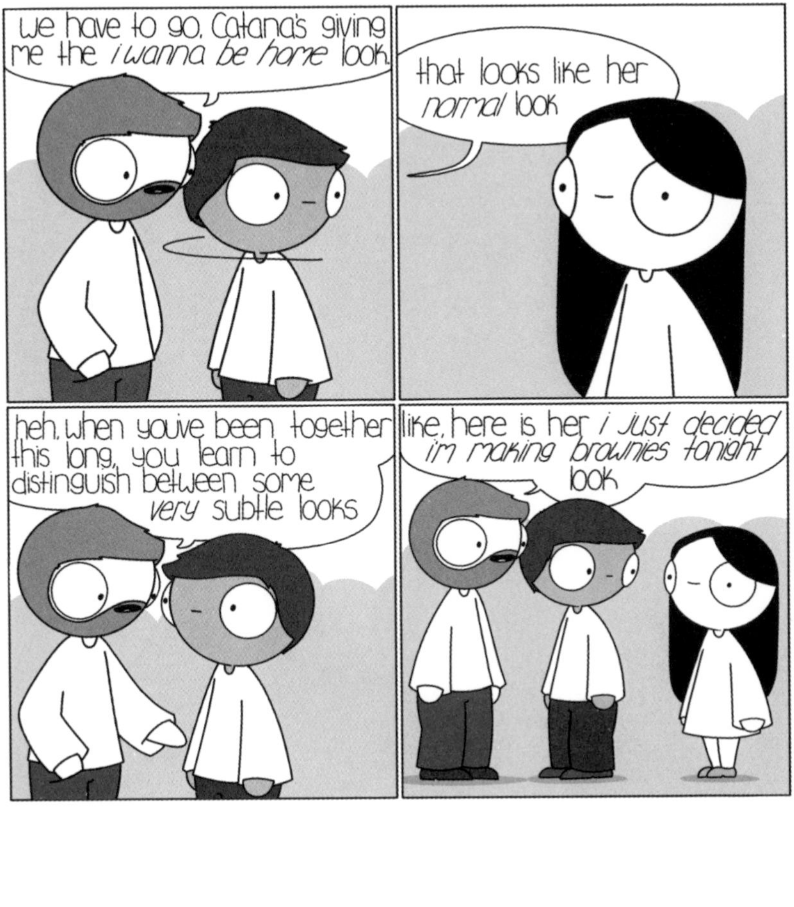
we have to go. Catana's giving me the *i wanna be home* look.
that looks like her *normal* look
heh. when you've been together this long, you learn to distinguish between some *very* subtle looks
like, here is her *i just decided i'm making brownies tonight* look

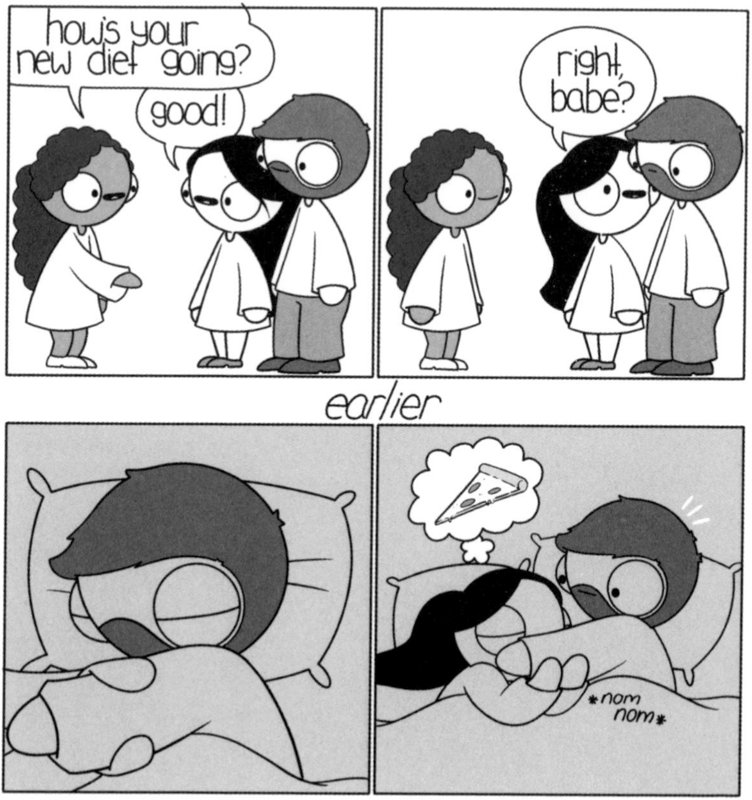
how's your new diet going?
good!
right, babe?
earlier
nom nom

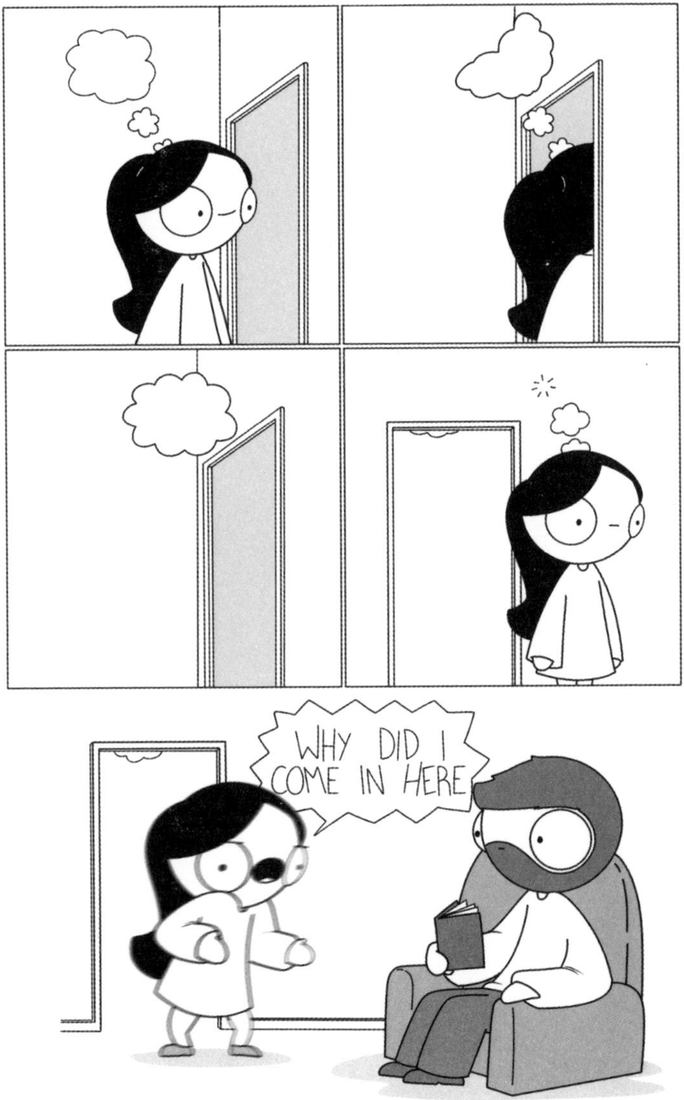
WHY DID I
COME IN HERE

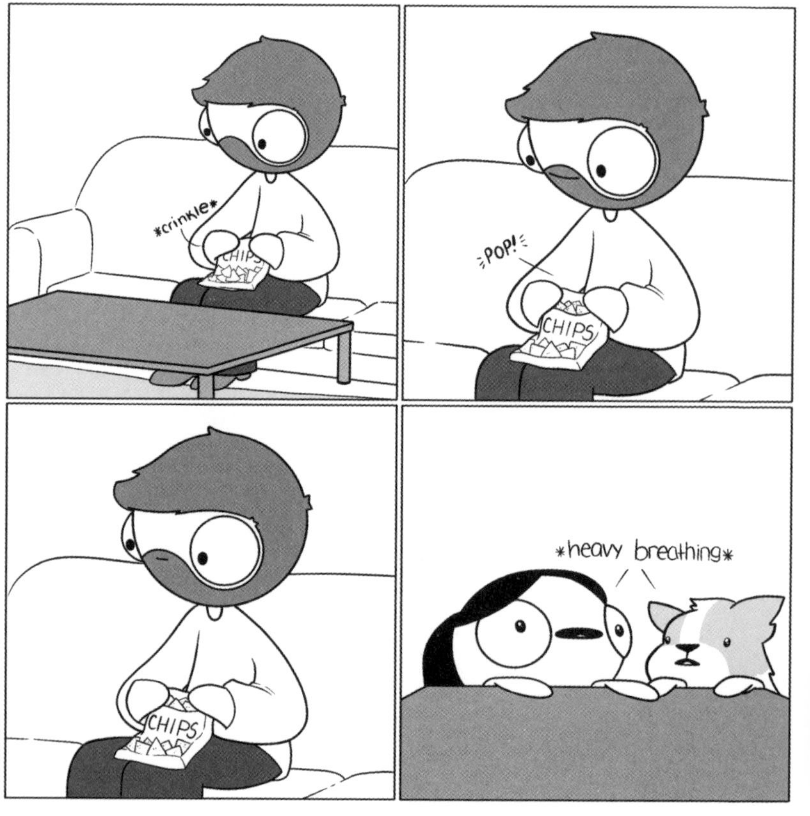
crinkle
CHIPS
POP!
CHIPS
CHIPS
heavy breathing

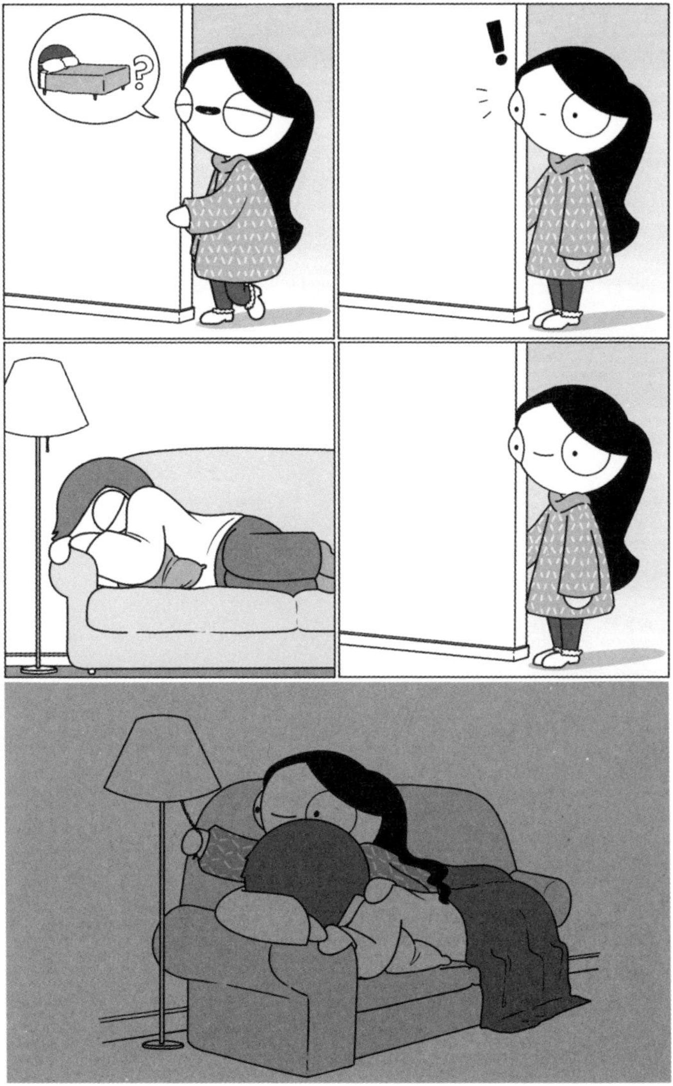

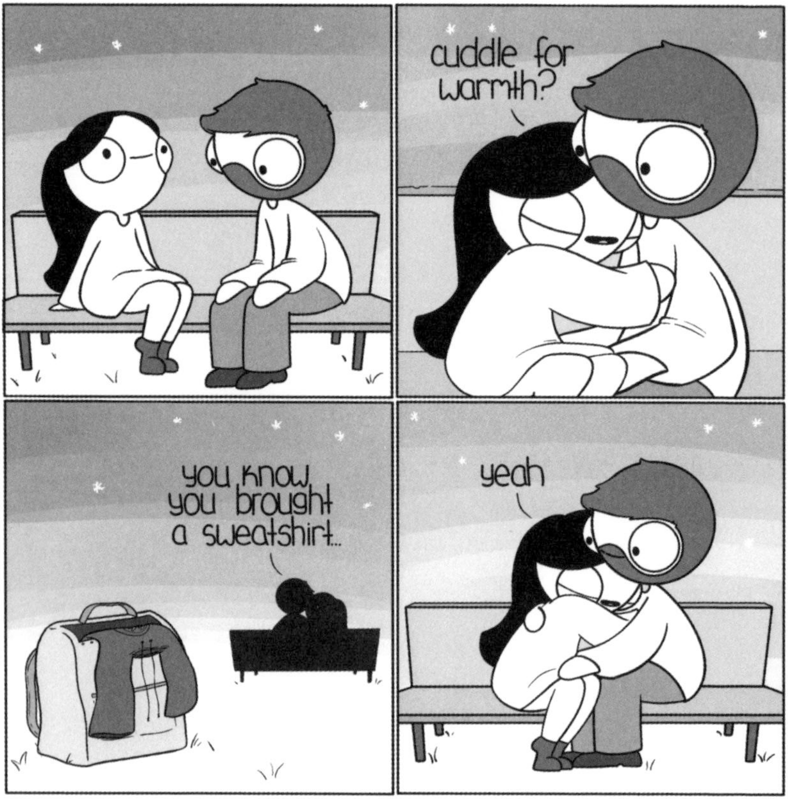
cuddle for warmth?
you know you brought a sweatshirt...
yeah

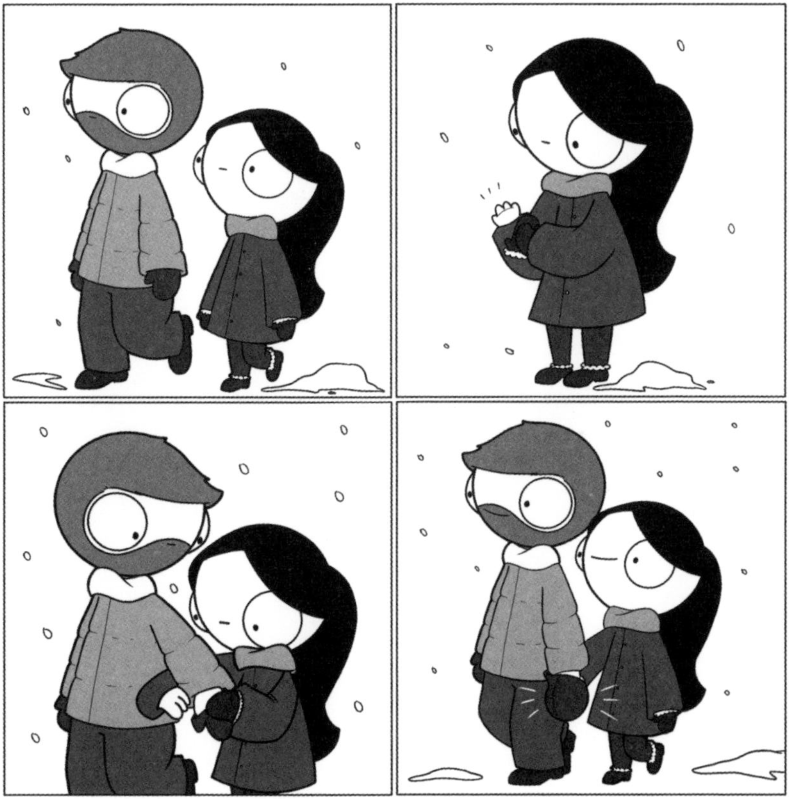

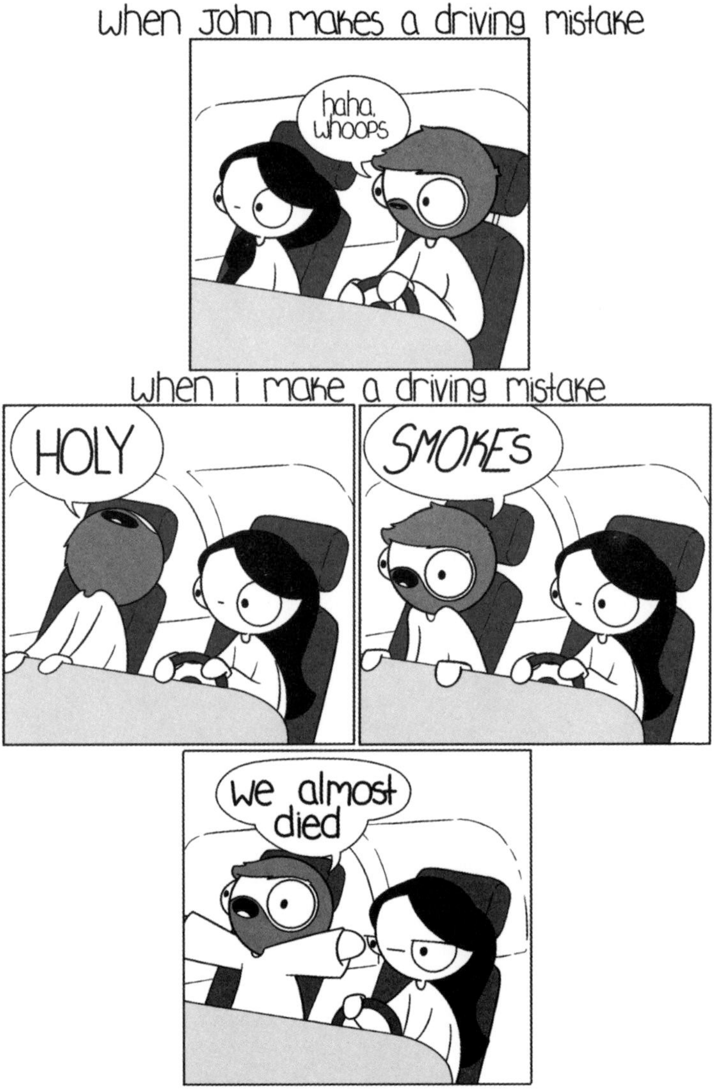
when John makes a driving mistake
haha, whoops
when i make a driving mistake
HOLY
SMOKES
we almost died

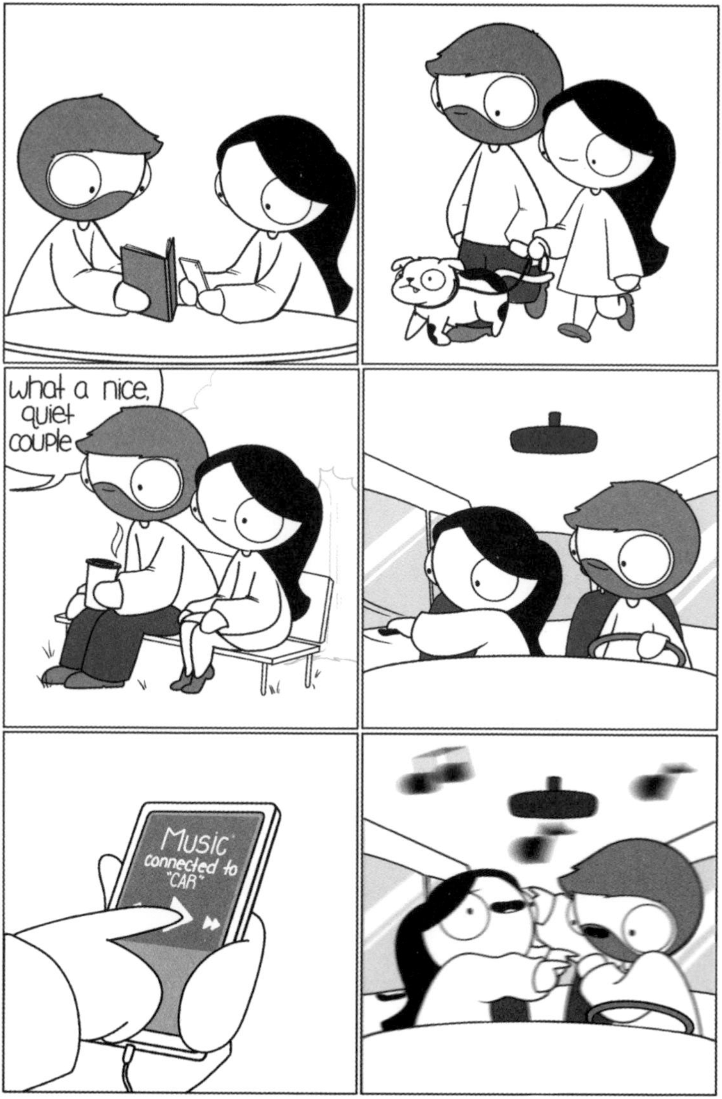
what a nice, quiet couple
Music
connected to "CAR"

Types of hand holds
the mitten
the classic
the cold girlfriend
the just-watched-a-horror-movie
meechh

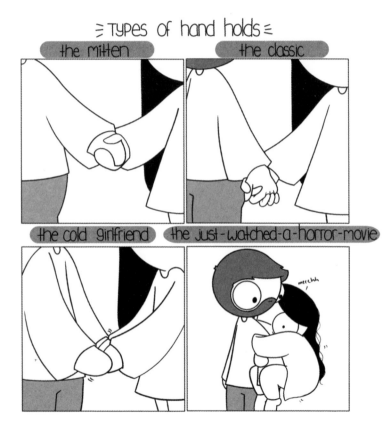

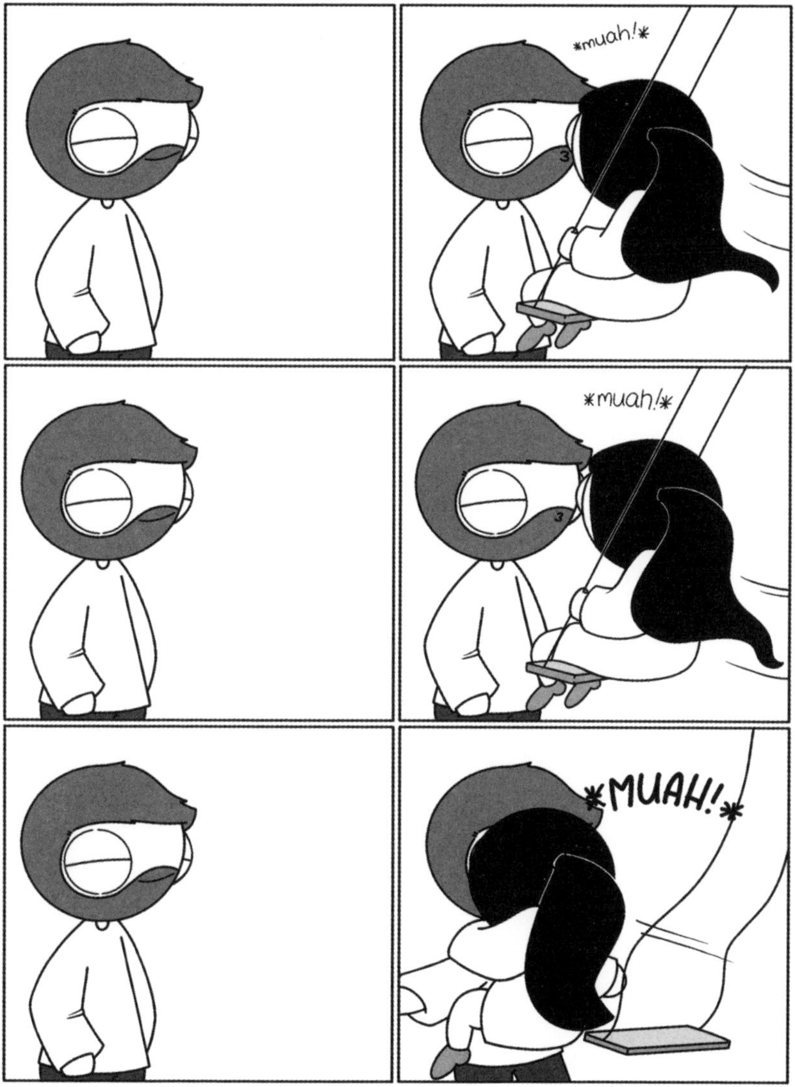
muah!
muah!
MUAH!

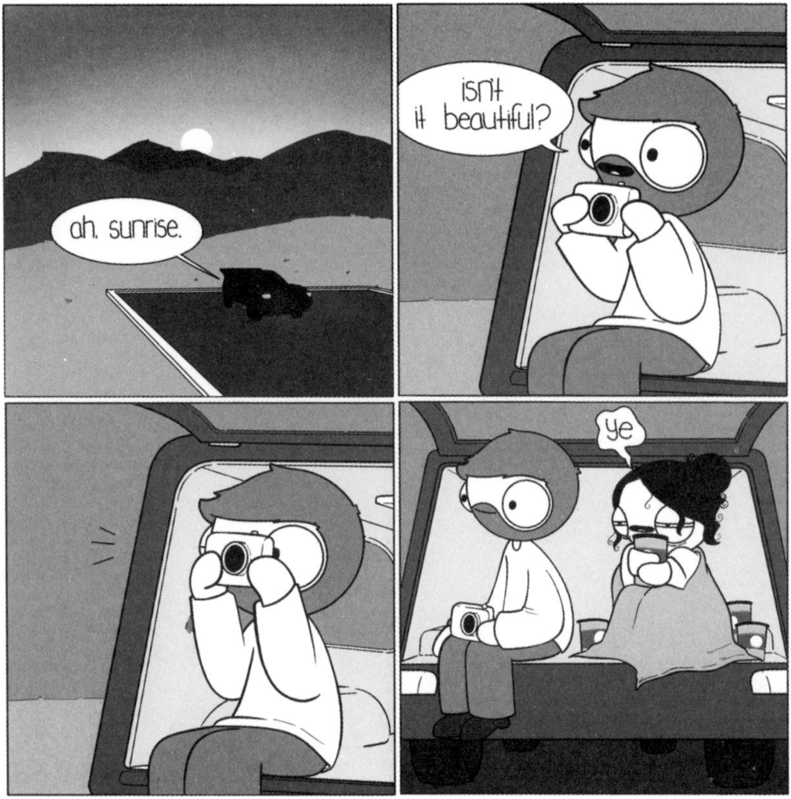
ah, sunrise.
isn't it beautiful?
ye

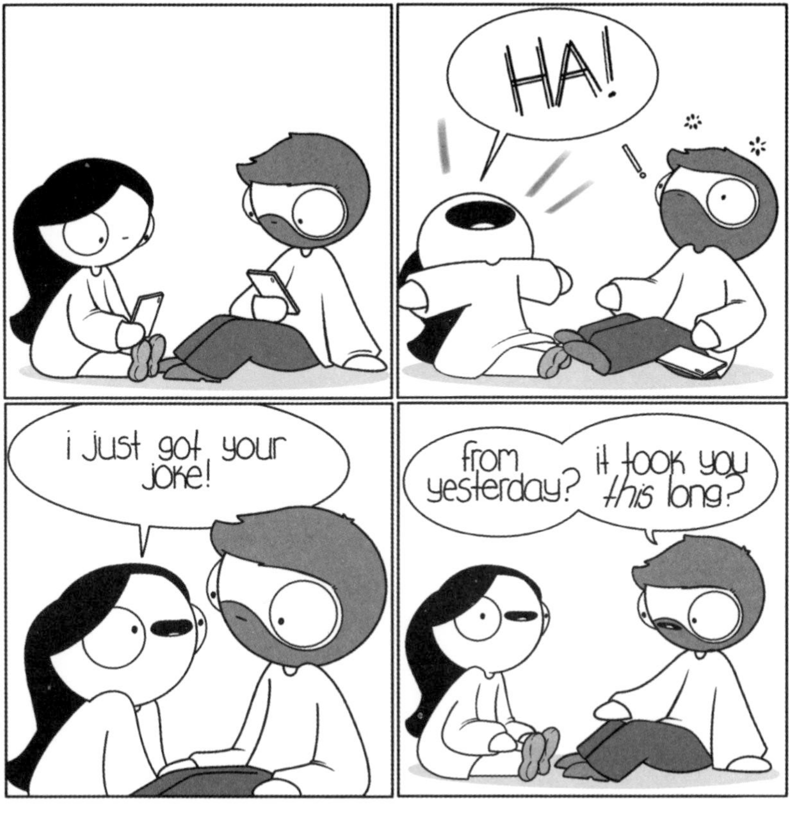
HA!
!
i just got your joke!
from yesterday?
it took you *this* long?

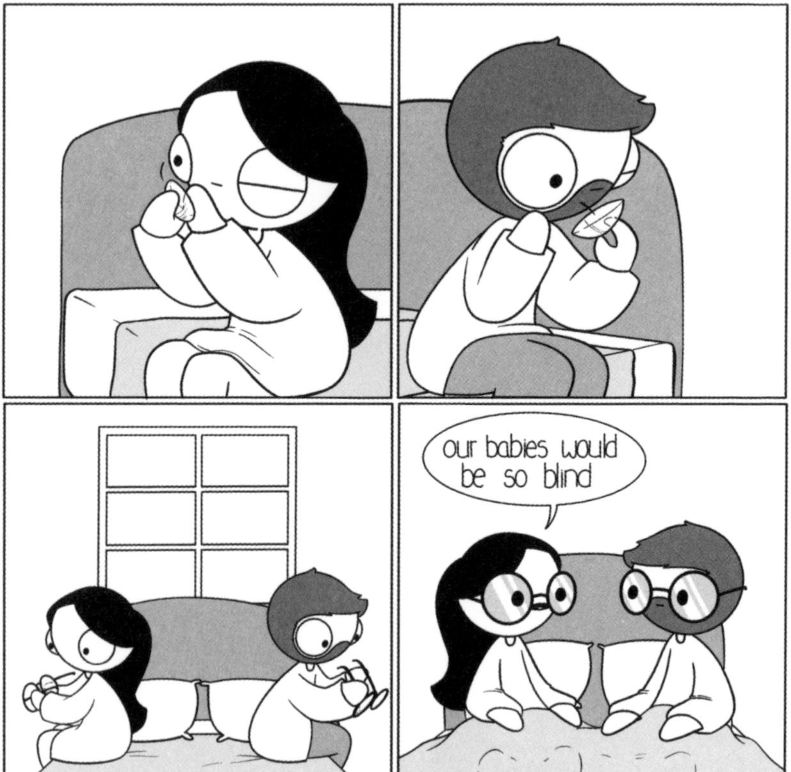
our babies would be so blind

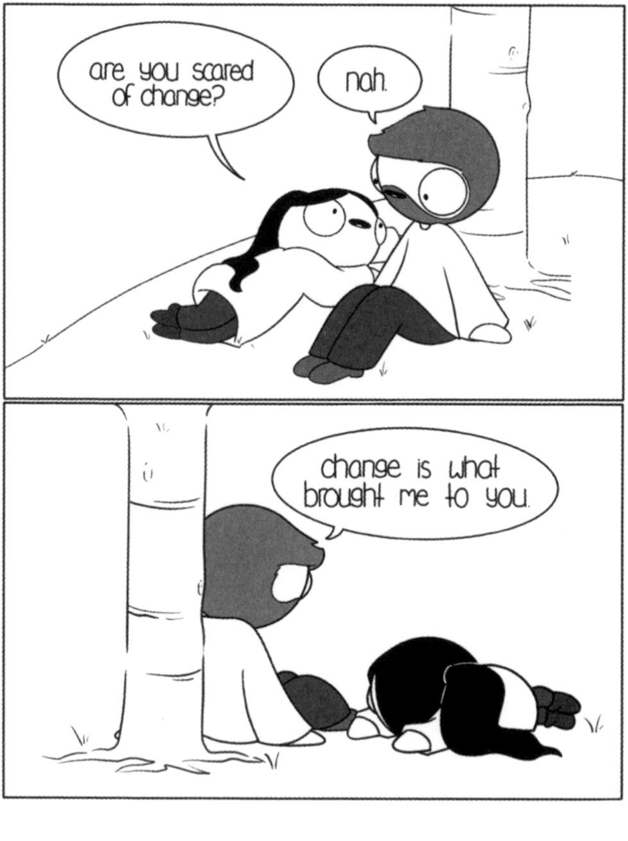
are you scared
of change?
nah.
change is what
brought me to you.

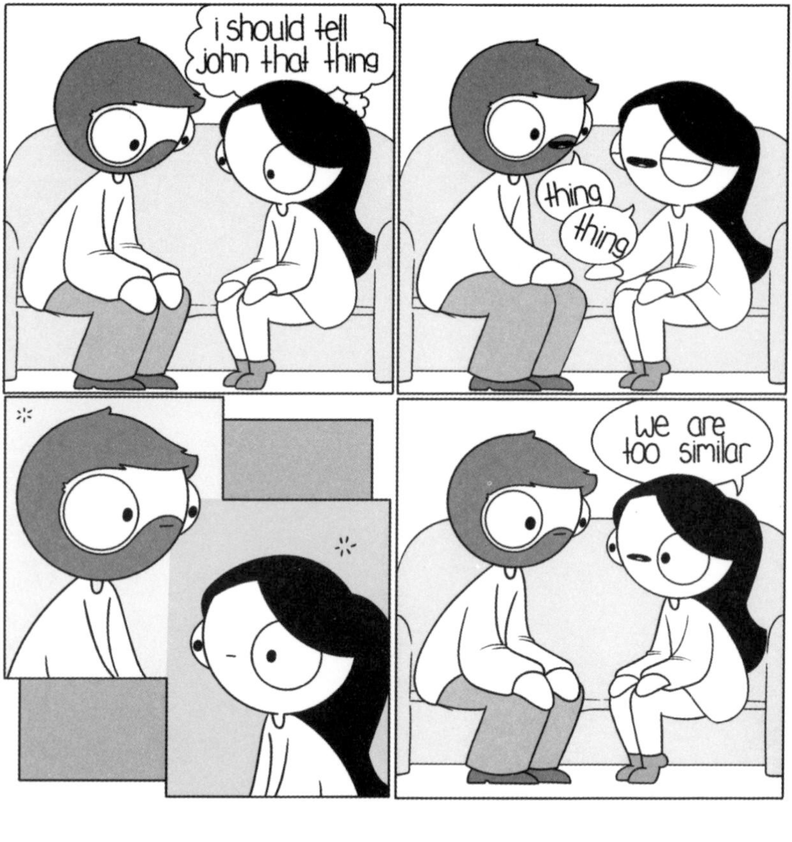
i should tell john that thing
thing
thing
we are too similar

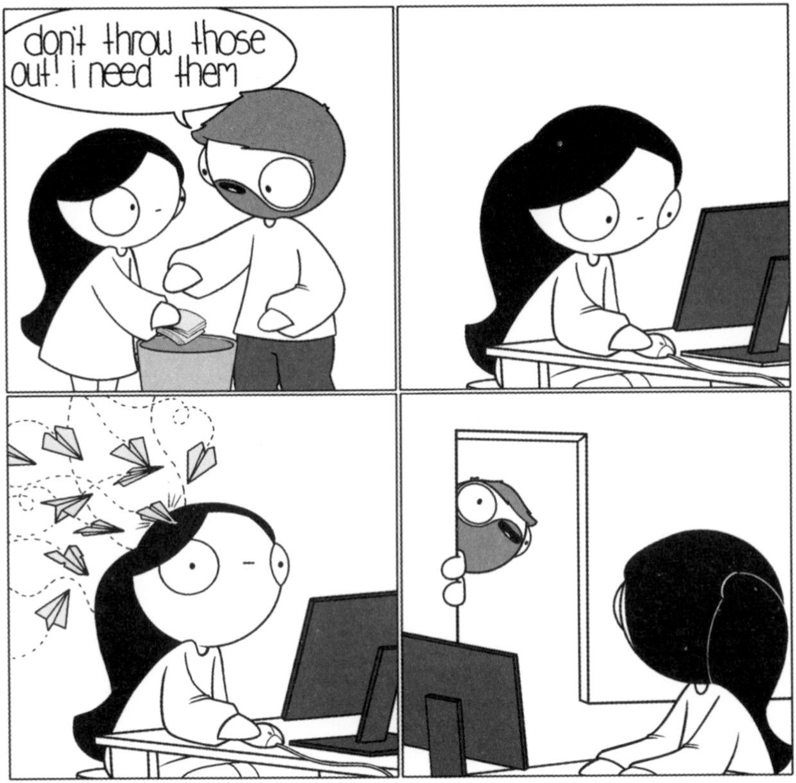
don't throw those out! i need them

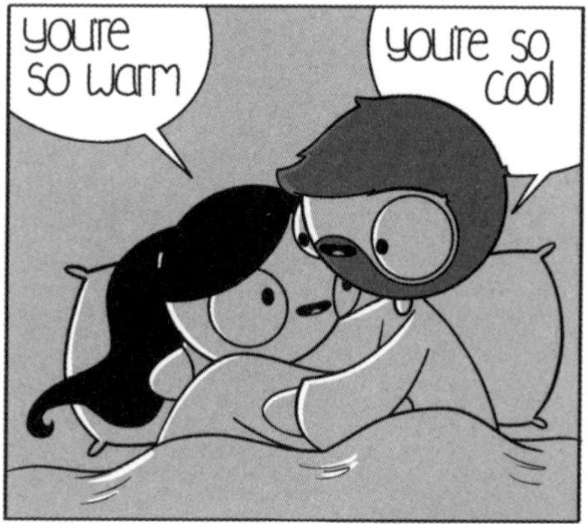
you're
so warm
you're so
cool

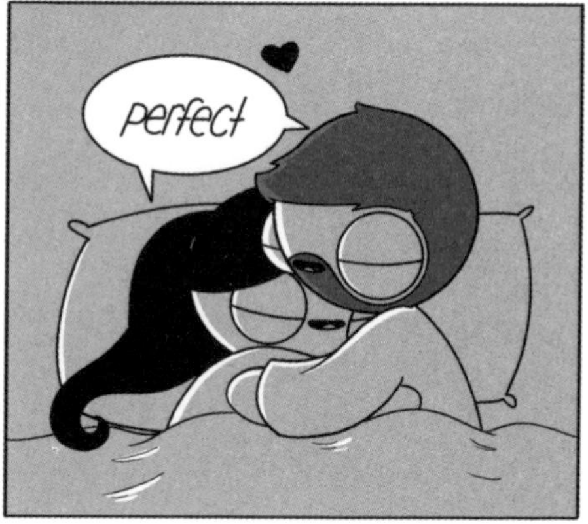
perfect

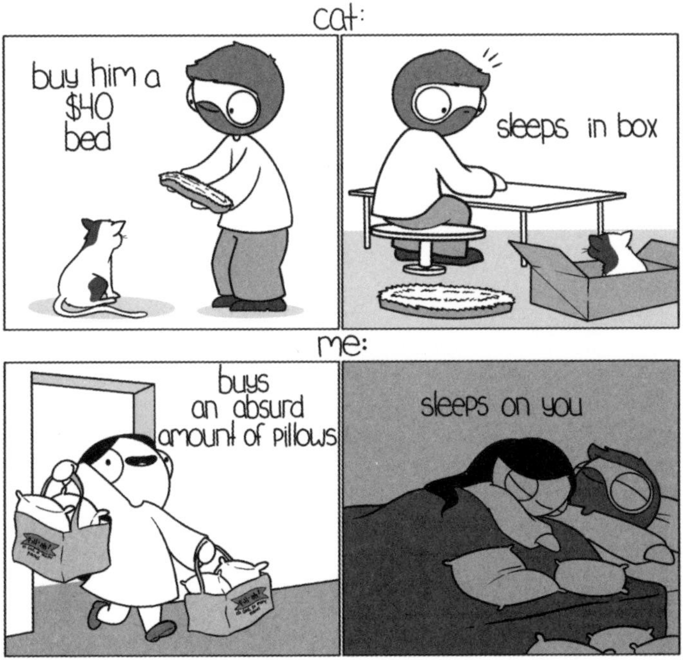
cat:
buy him a $40 bed
sleeps in box
me:
buys an absurd amount of pillows
sleeps on you

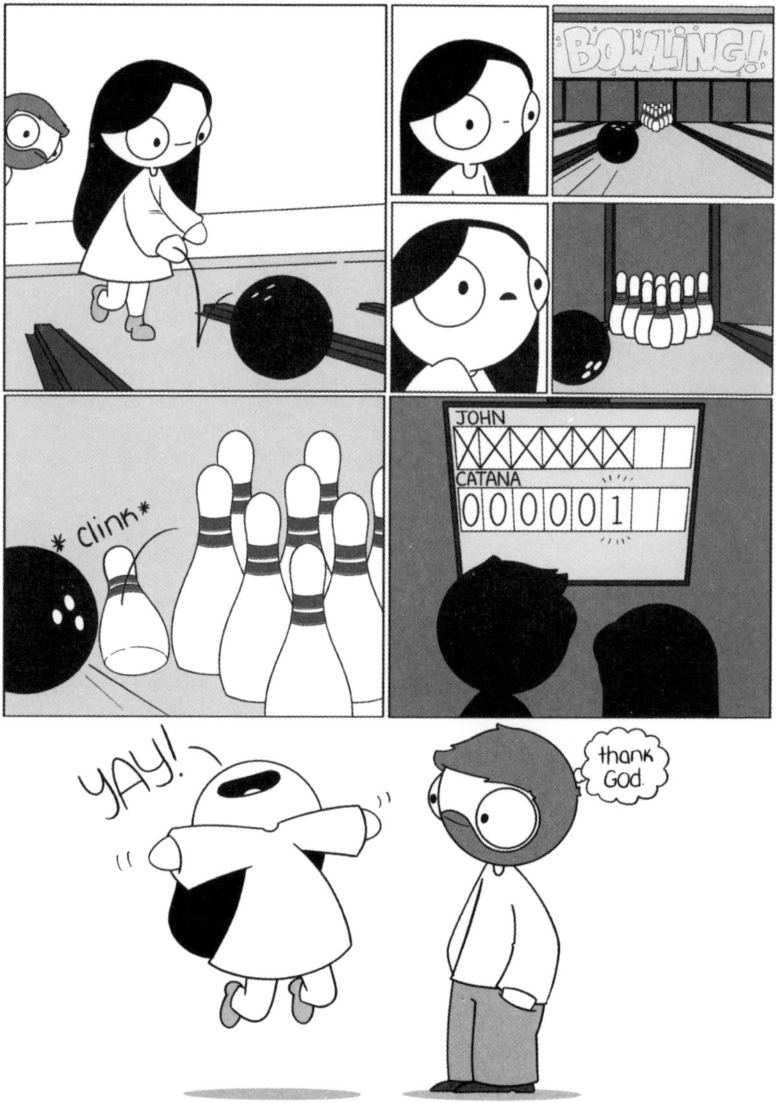
BOWLING!
JOHN
CATANA
0 0 0 0 0 1
clink
YAY!
thank God.

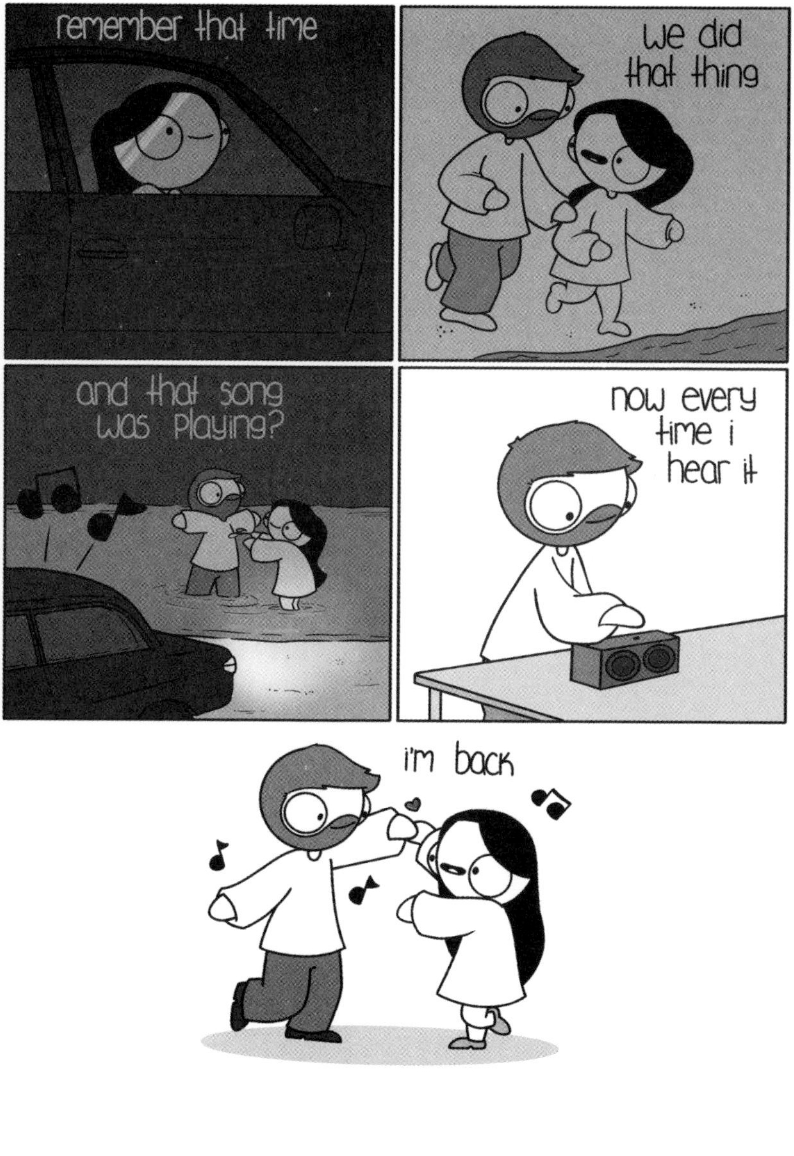
remember that time
we did that thing
and that song was playing?
now every time i hear it
i'm back

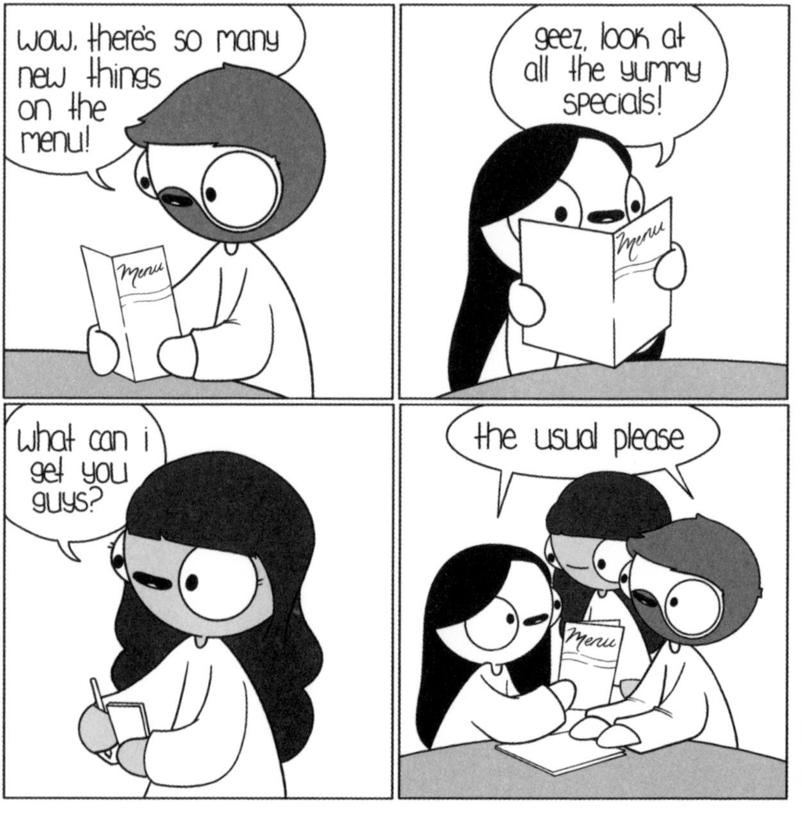
wow, there's so many new things on the menu!
Menu
geez, look at all the yummy specials!
Menu
what can i get you guys?
the usual please
Menu

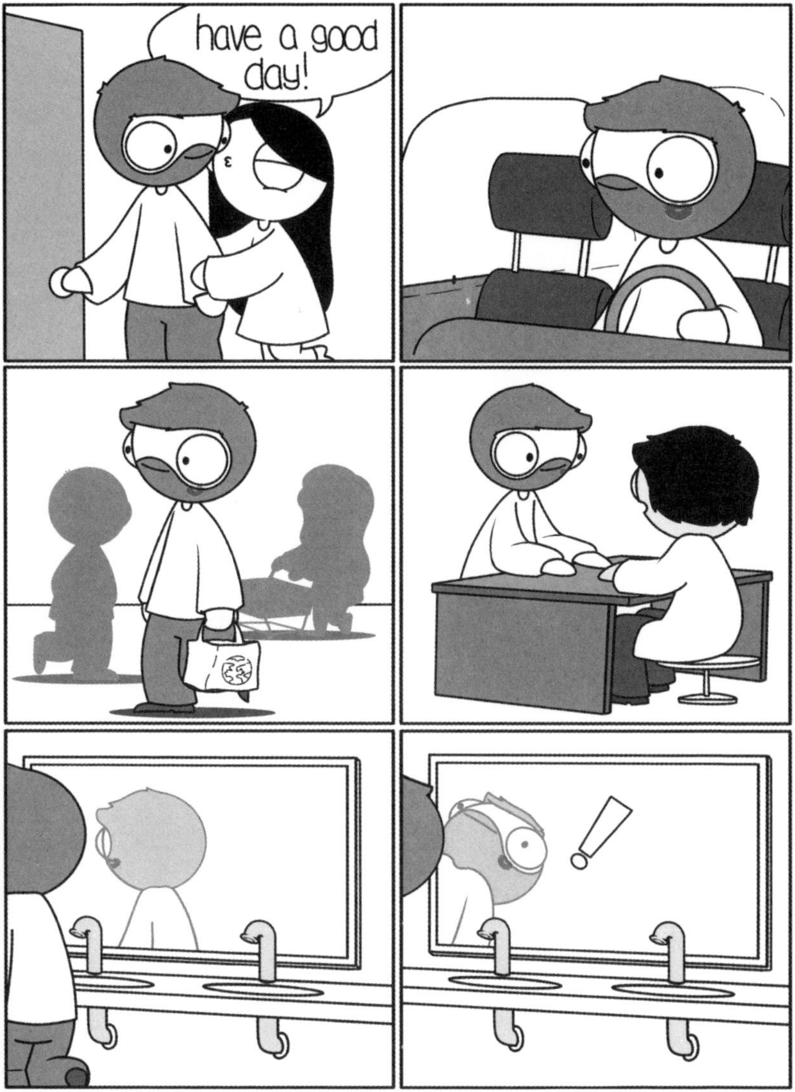
have a good day!
!

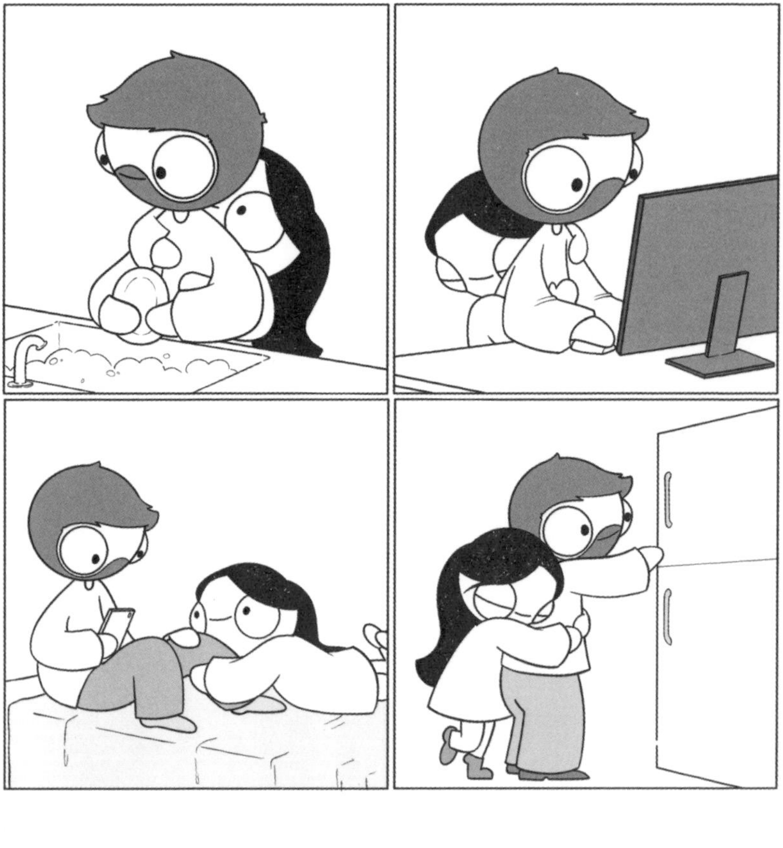

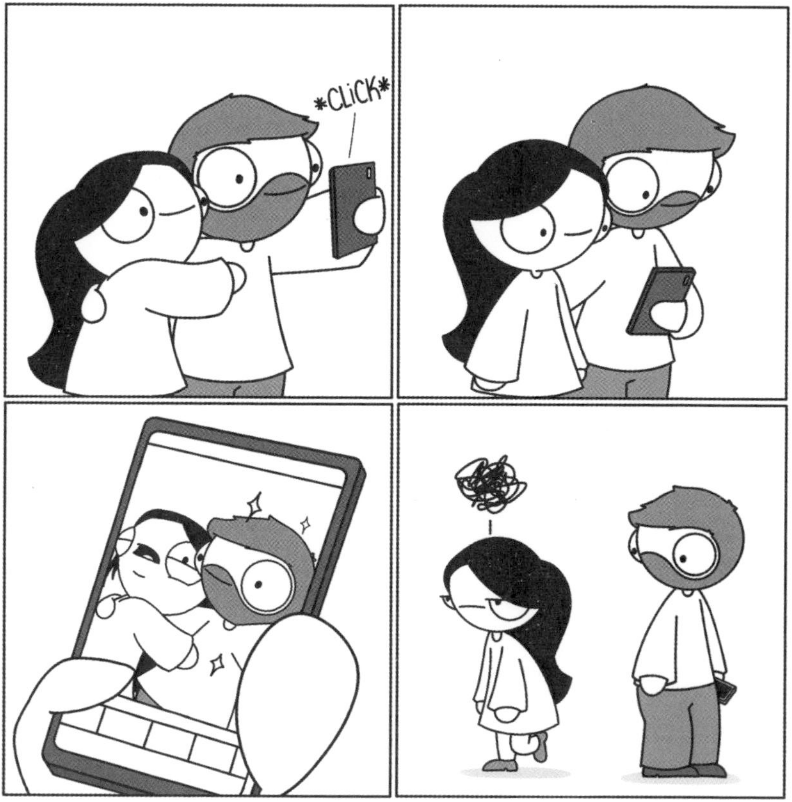
CLICK

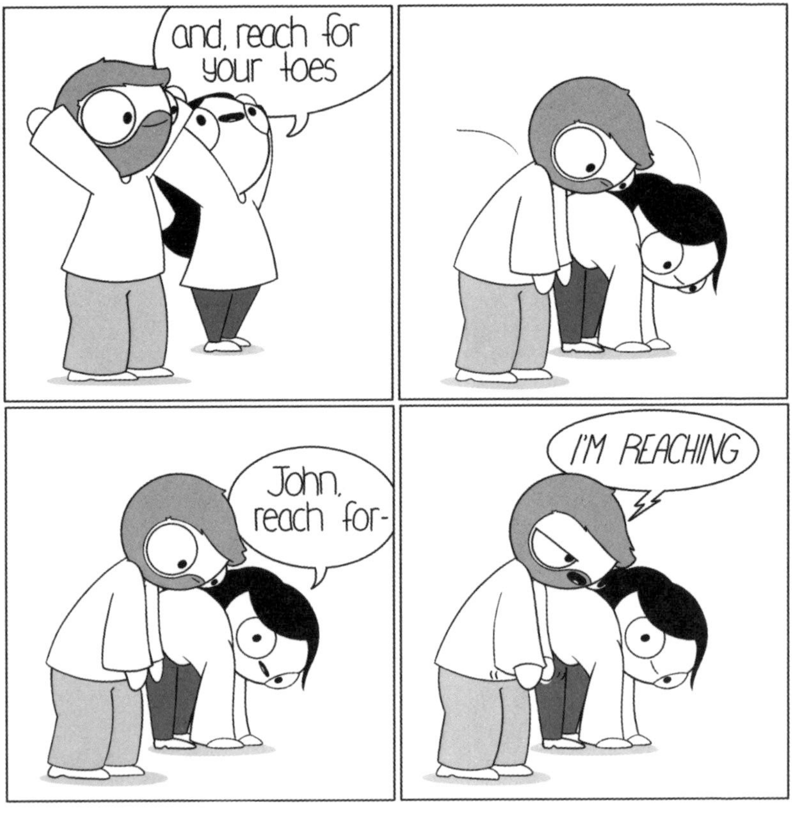
and, reach for your toes
John, reach for-
I'M REACHING

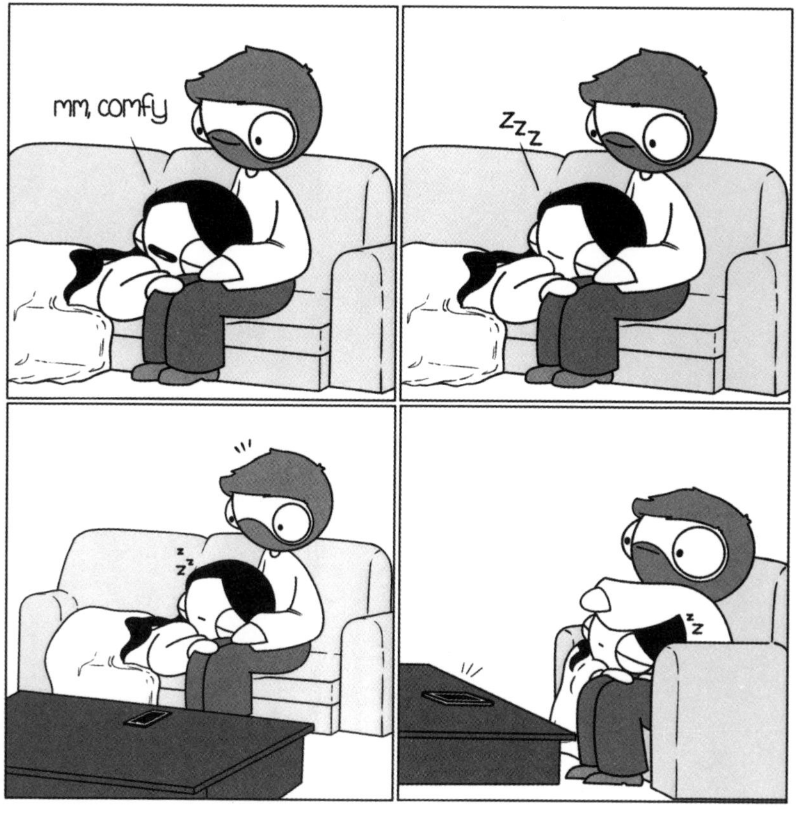
mm, comfy
zzz
z z
z z

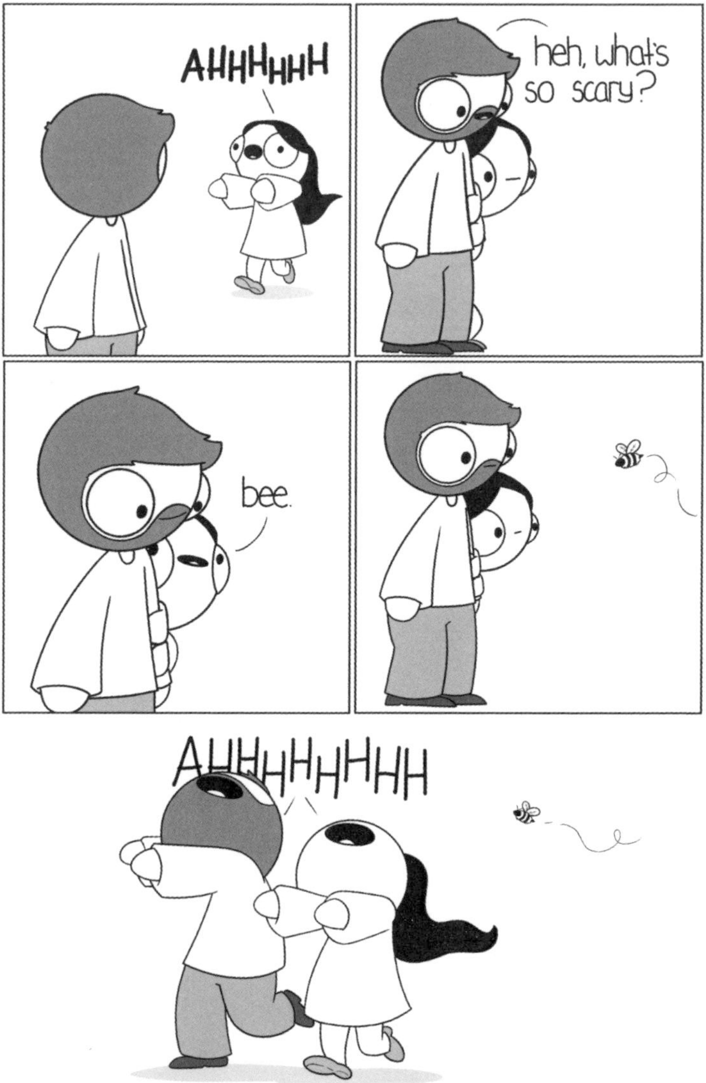
AHHHHHH
heh, what's so scary?
bee.
AHHHHHHHHH

me as a ghost:

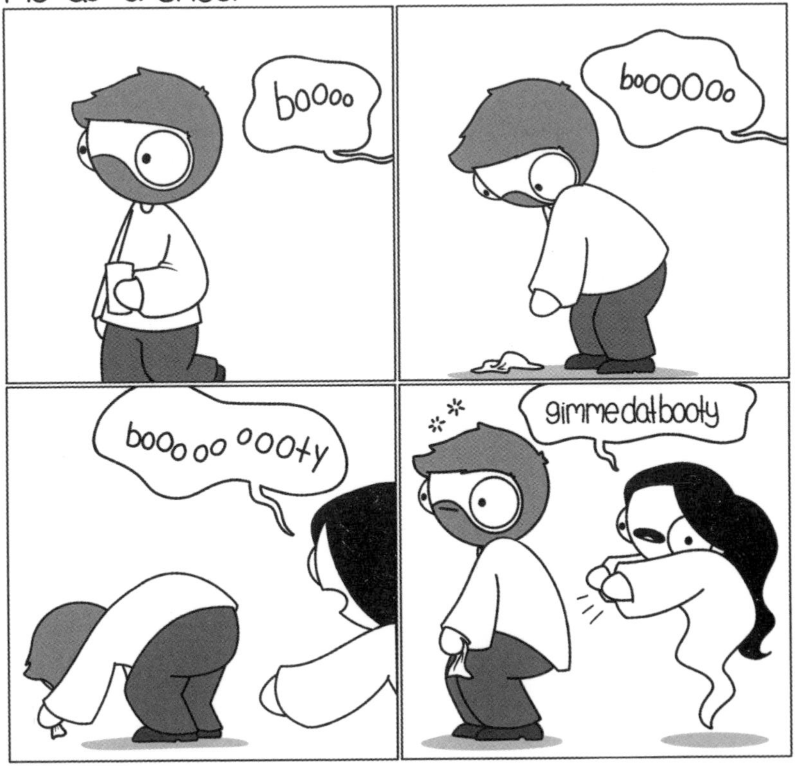
boOoo
boOOOOo
boOo oo oOOty
gimmedatbooty

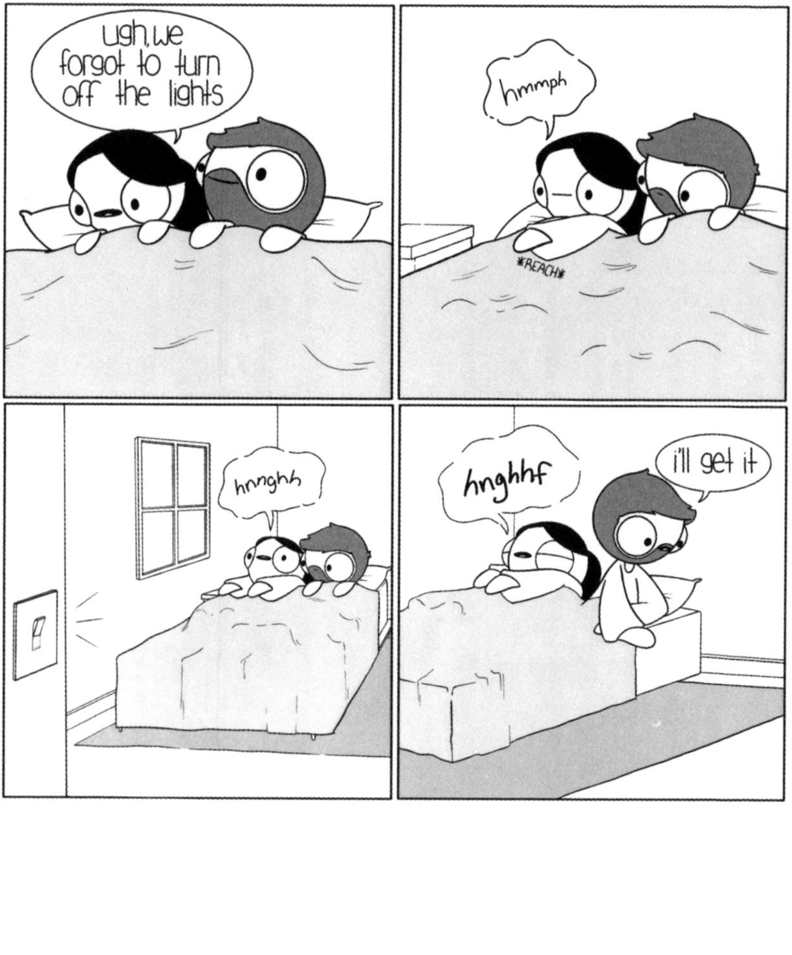
ugh, we forgot to turn off the lights
hmmph
REACH
hnnghh
hnghhf
i'll get it

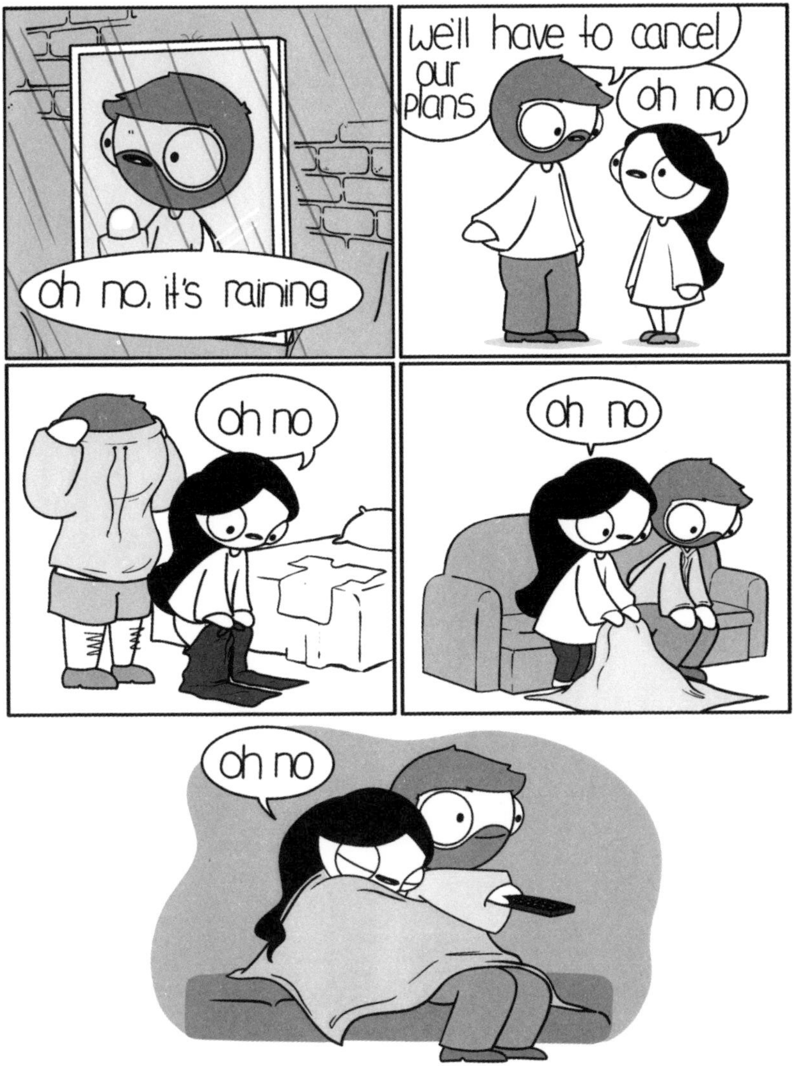
oh no, it's raining
we'll have to cancel our plans
oh no
oh no
oh no
oh no

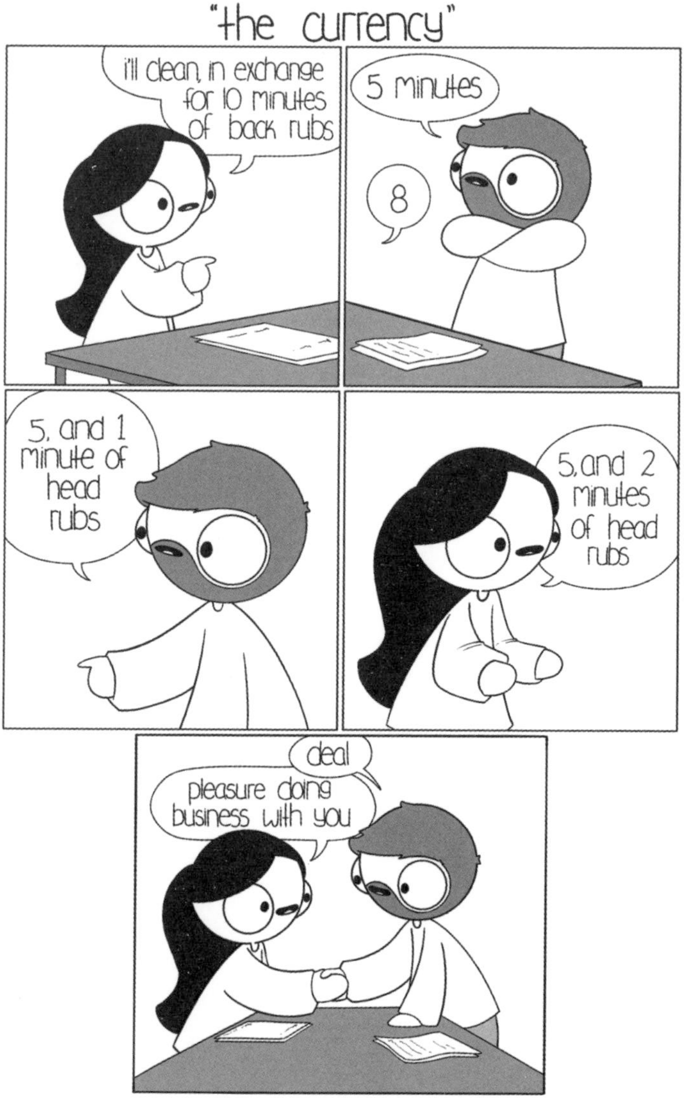
"the currency"
i'll clean, in exchange for 10 minutes of back rubs
5 minutes
8
5, and 1 minute of head rubs
5, and 2 minutes of head rubs
pleasure doing business with you
deal

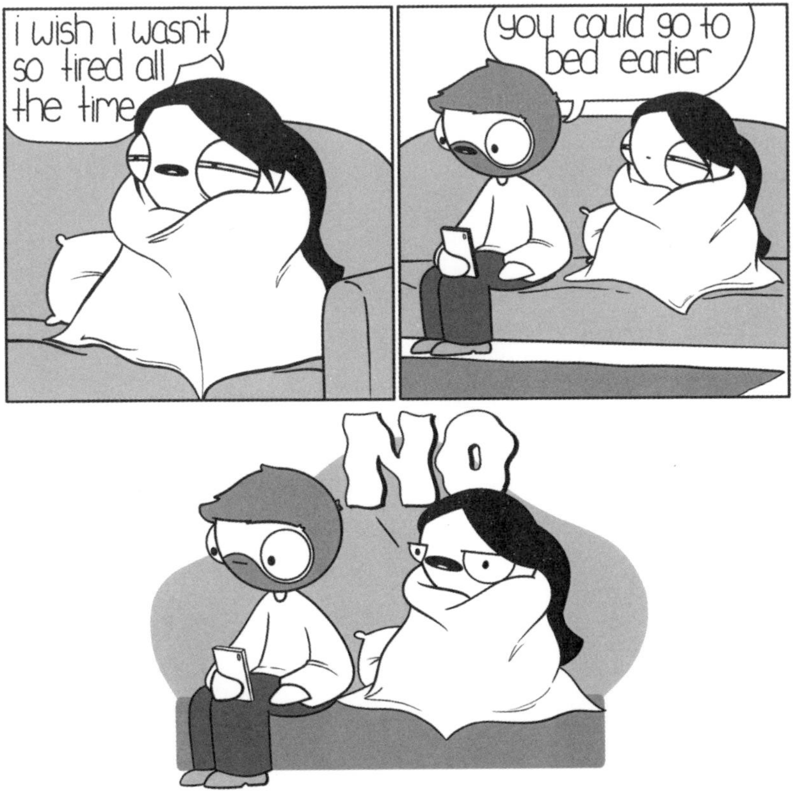
i wish i wasn't so tired all the time
you could go to bed earlier
NO

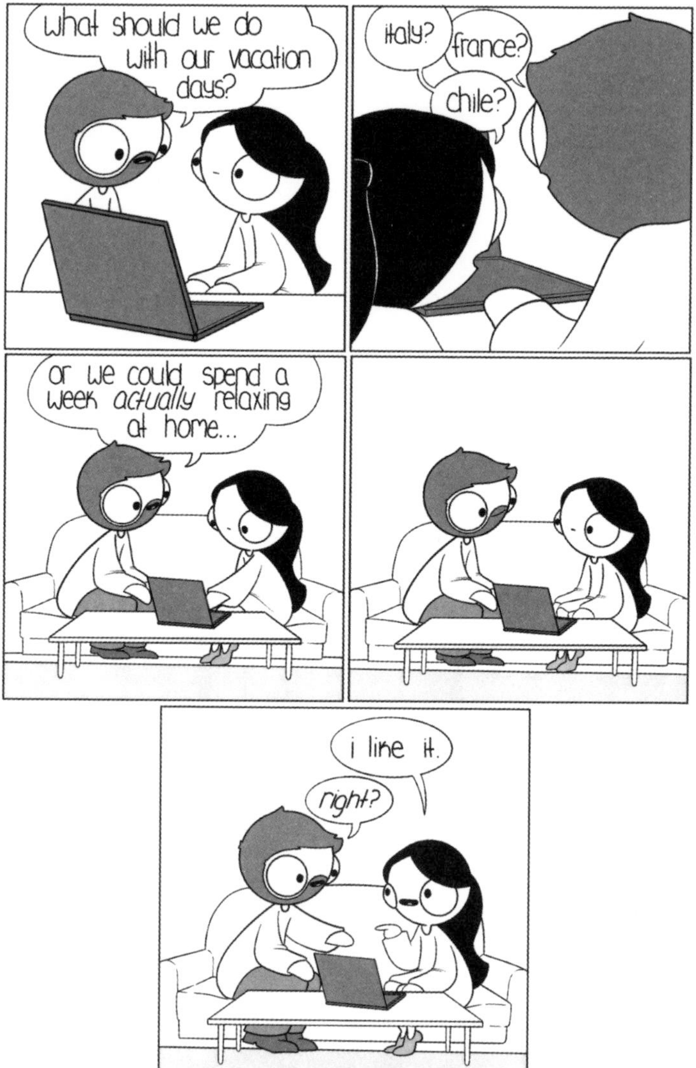
what should we do with our vacation days?
italy?
france?
chile?
or we could spend a week *actually* relaxing at home...
i like it.
right?

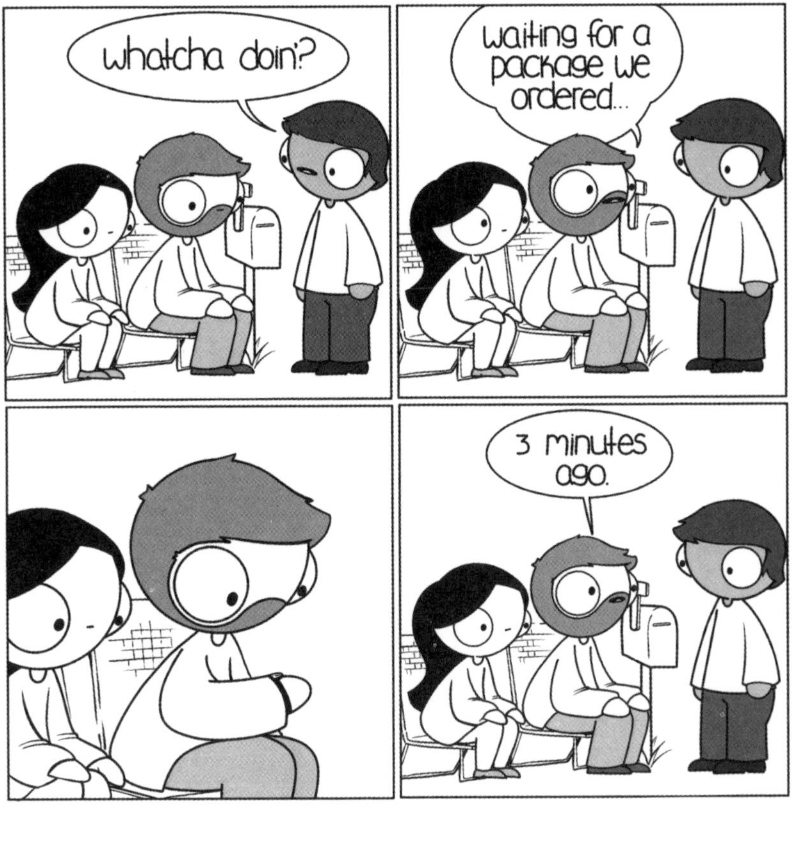
whatcha doin'?
waiting for a package we ordered...
3 minutes ago.

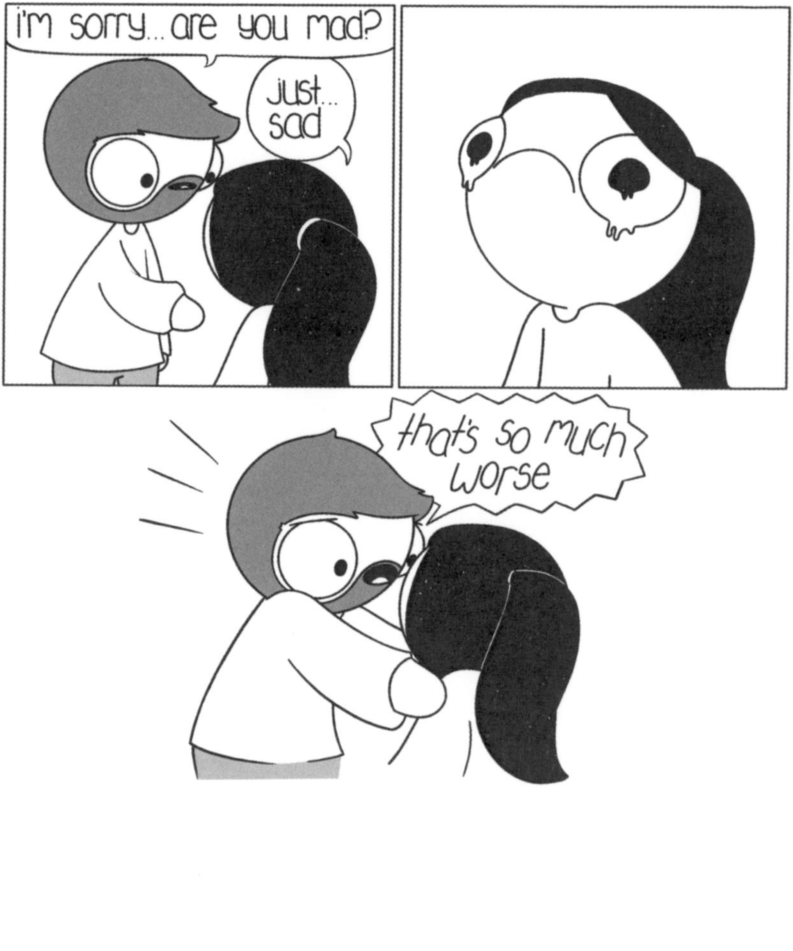
i'm sorry... are you mad?
just... sad
that's so much worse

"SUPPORT"

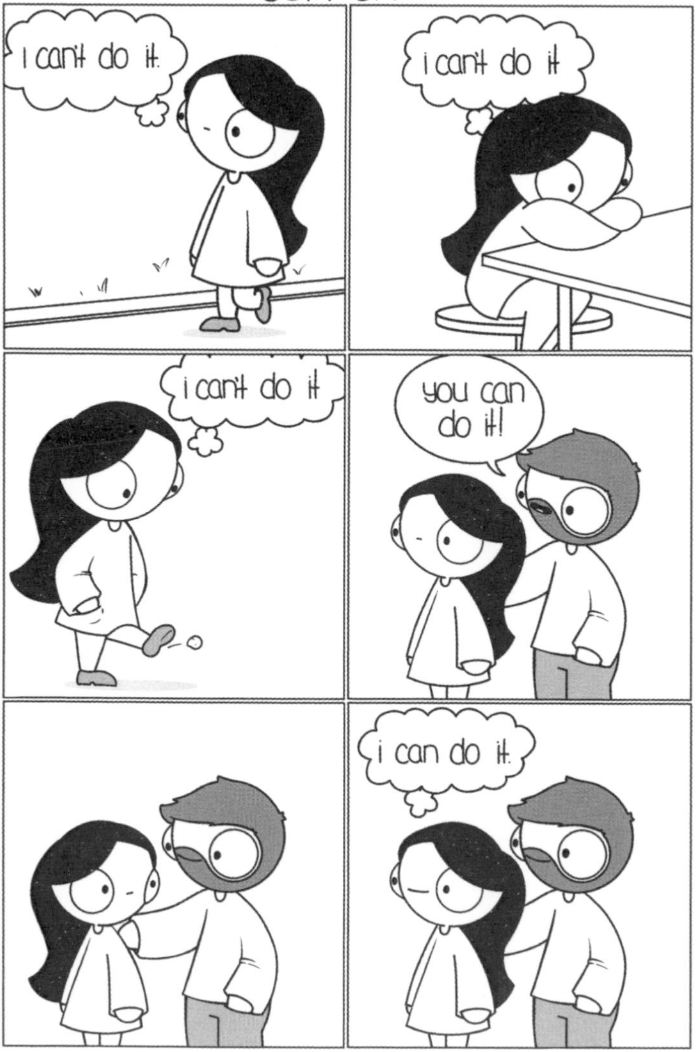
i can't do it.
i can't do it
i can't do it
you can do it!
i can do it.

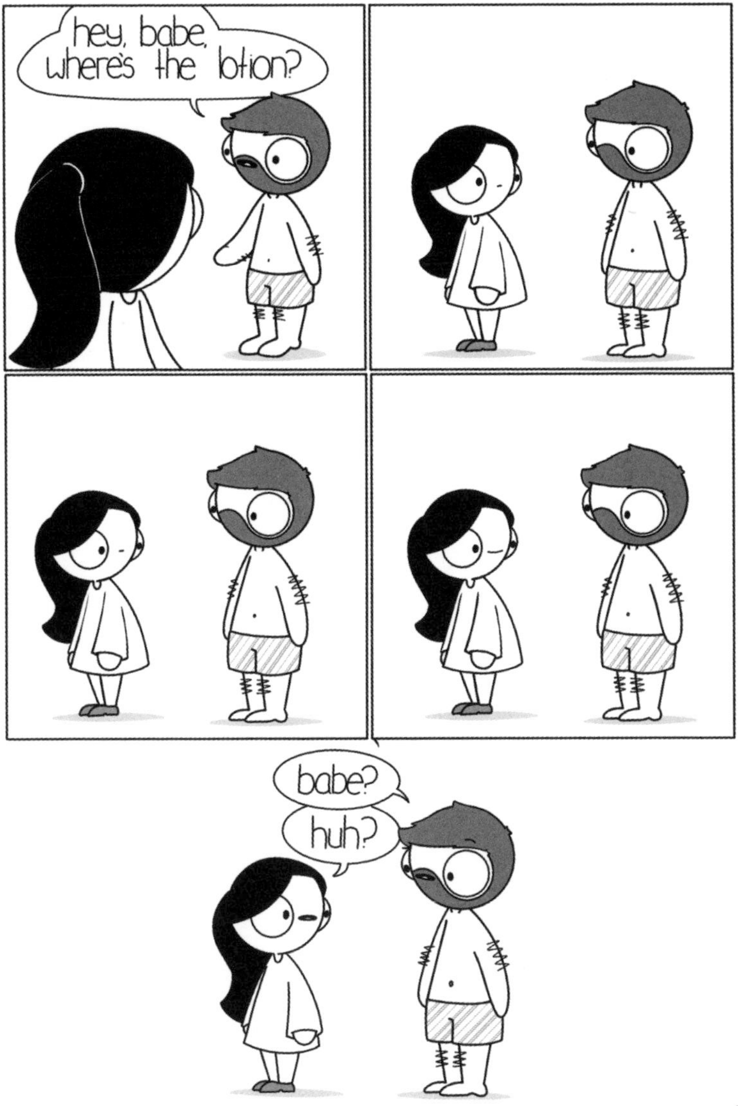
hey, babe,
where's the lotion?
babe?
huh?

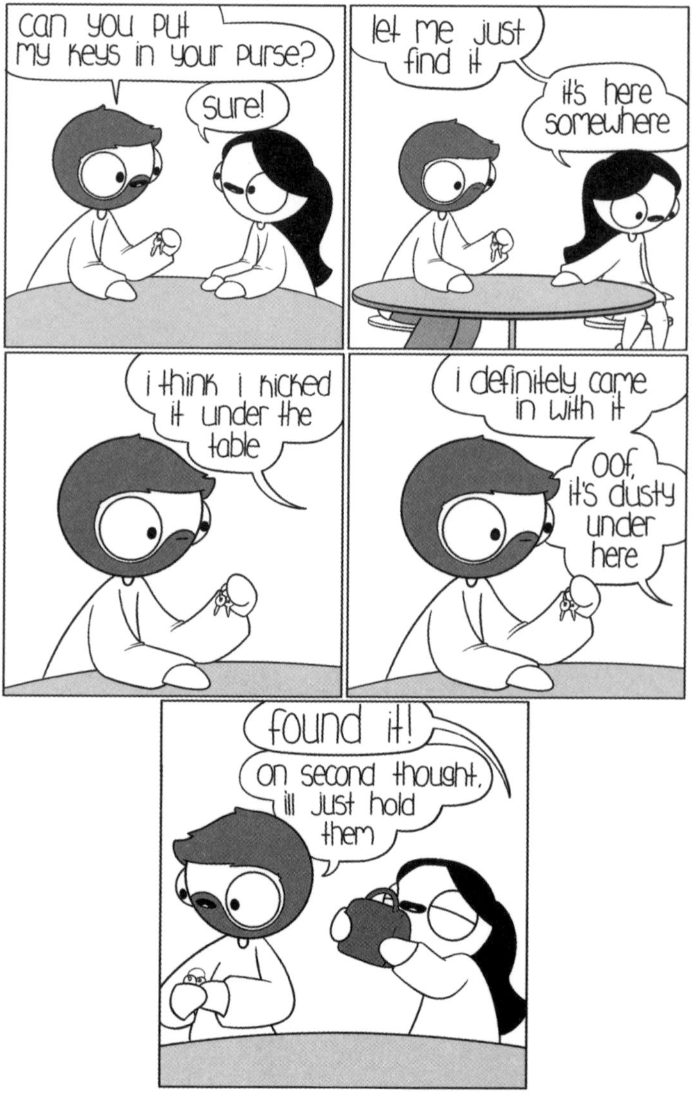
can you put my keys in your purse?
sure!
let me just find it
it's here somewhere
i think i kicked it under the table
i definitely came in with it
oof, it's dusty under here
found it!
on second thought, ill just hold them

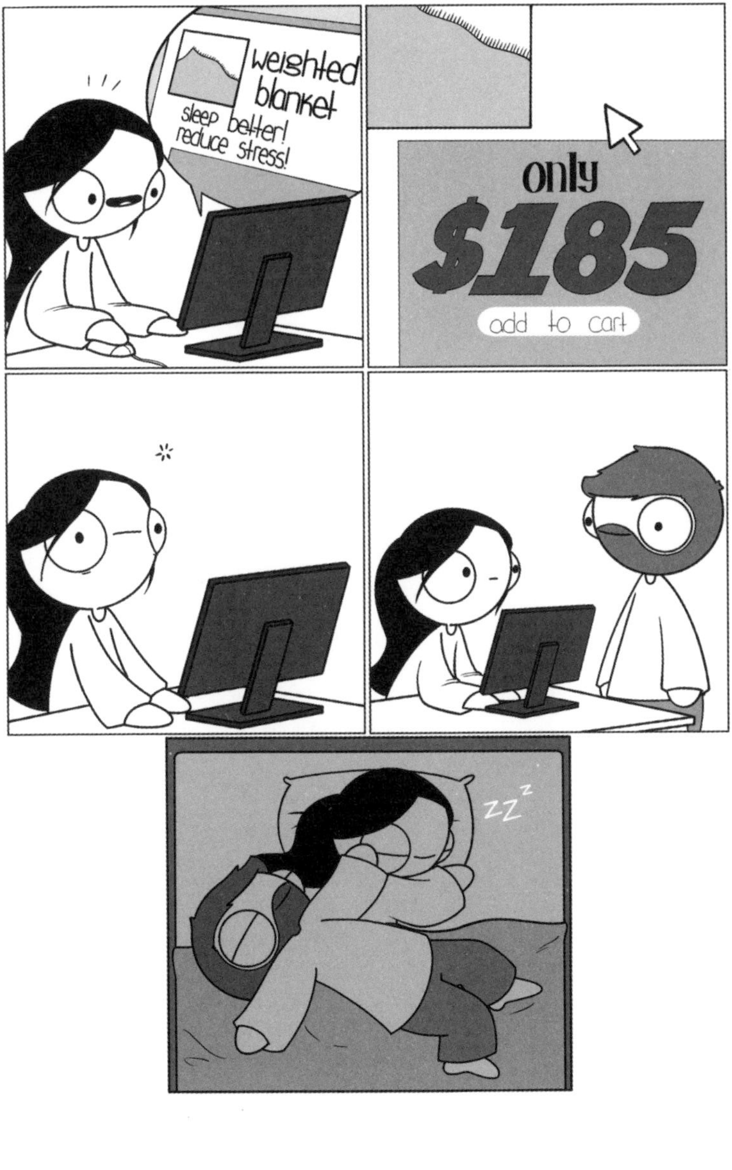
weighted blanket
sleep better!
reduce stress!
only
$185
add to cart
zzz

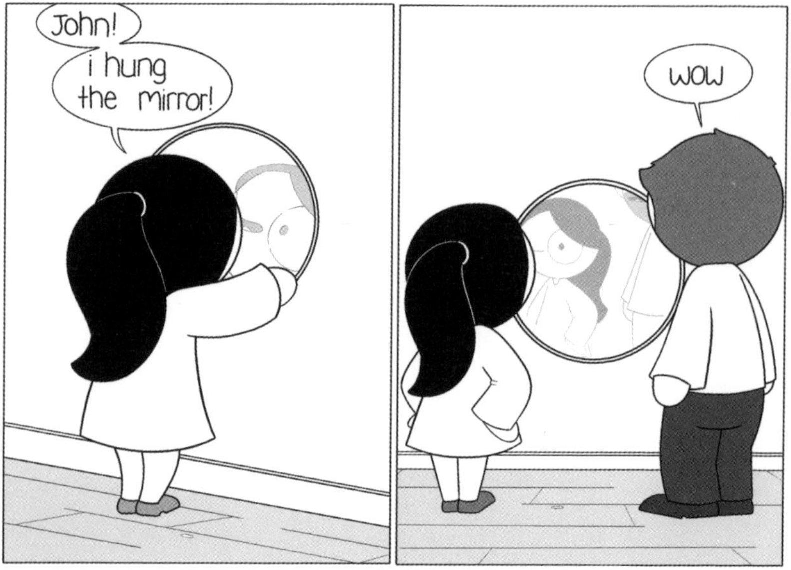
John!
i hung the mirror!
WOW

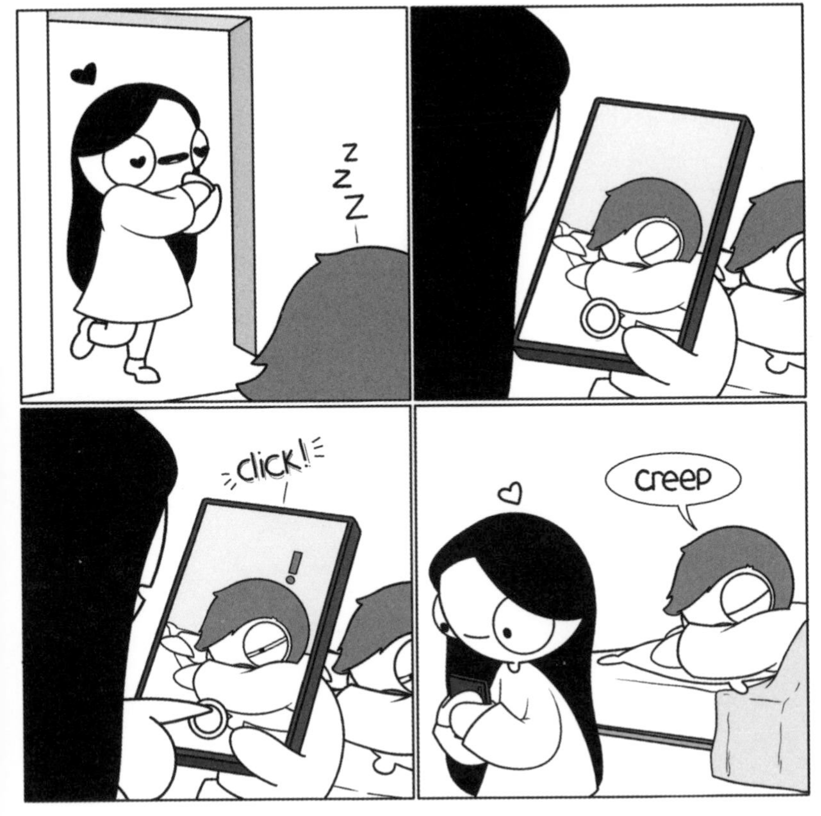
Z
Z
Z
CLICK!
!
creep

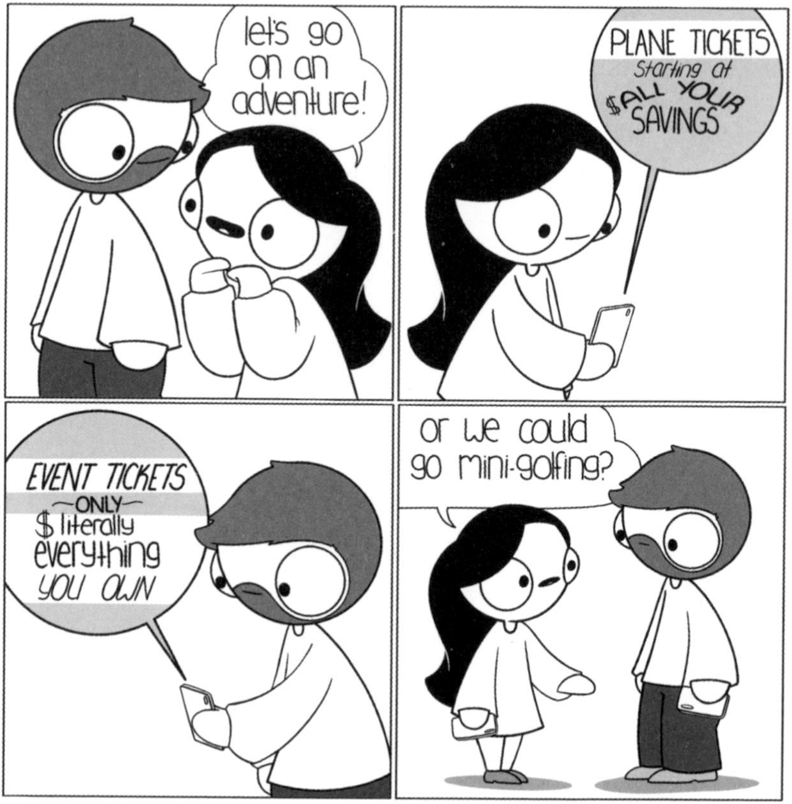
let's go
on an
adventure!
PLANE TICKETS
starting at
$ALL YOUR
SAVINGS
EVENT TICKETS
ONLY
$ literally
everything
YOU OWN
or we could
go mini-golfing?

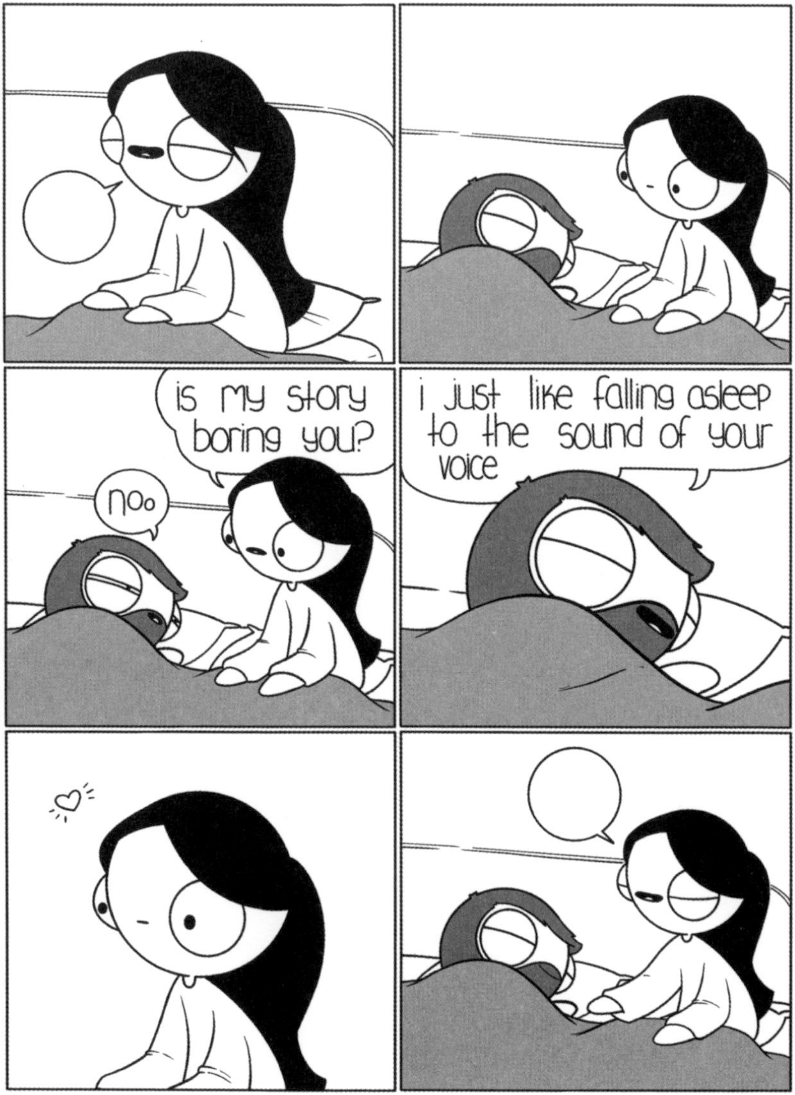
is my story boring you?
noo
i just like falling asleep to the sound of your voice

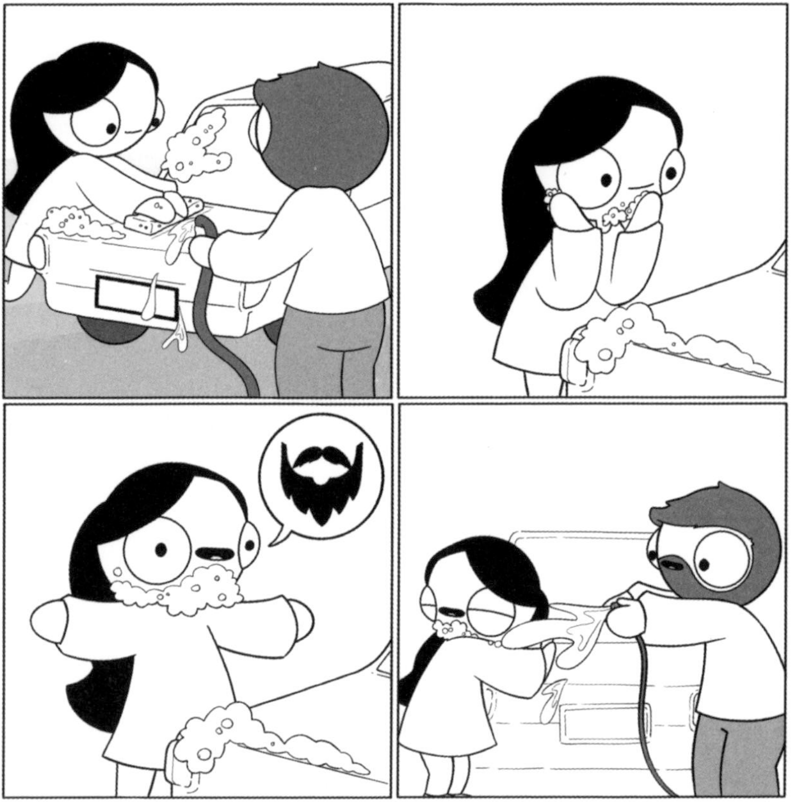

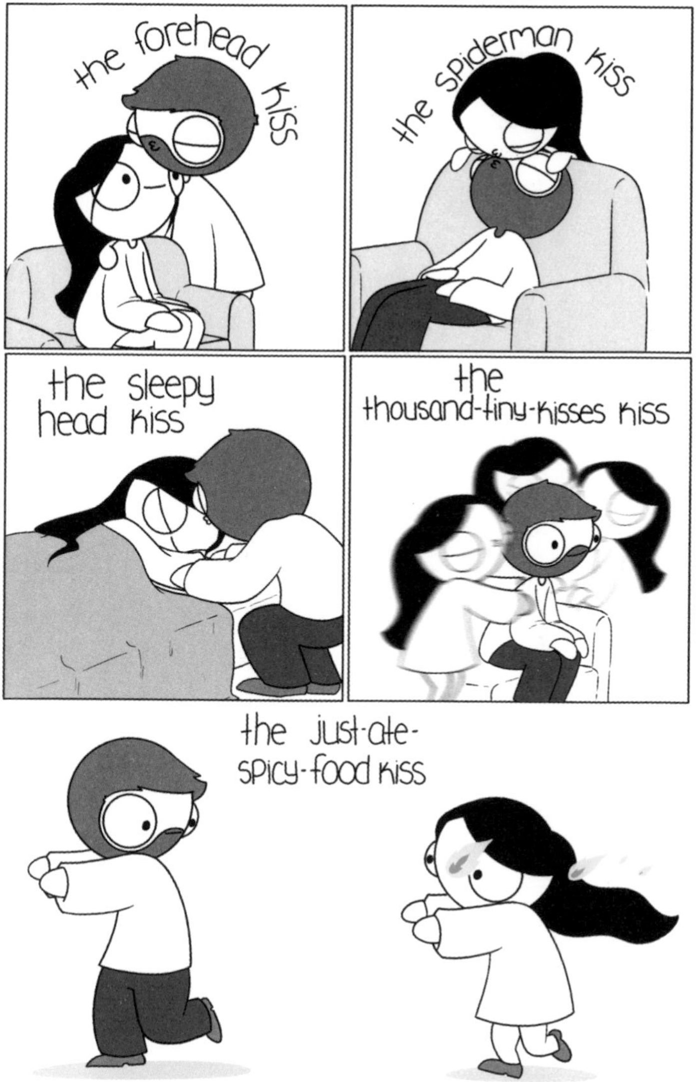
the forehead kiss
the spiderman kiss
the sleepy head kiss
the thousand-tiny-kisses kiss
the just-ate-spicy-food kiss

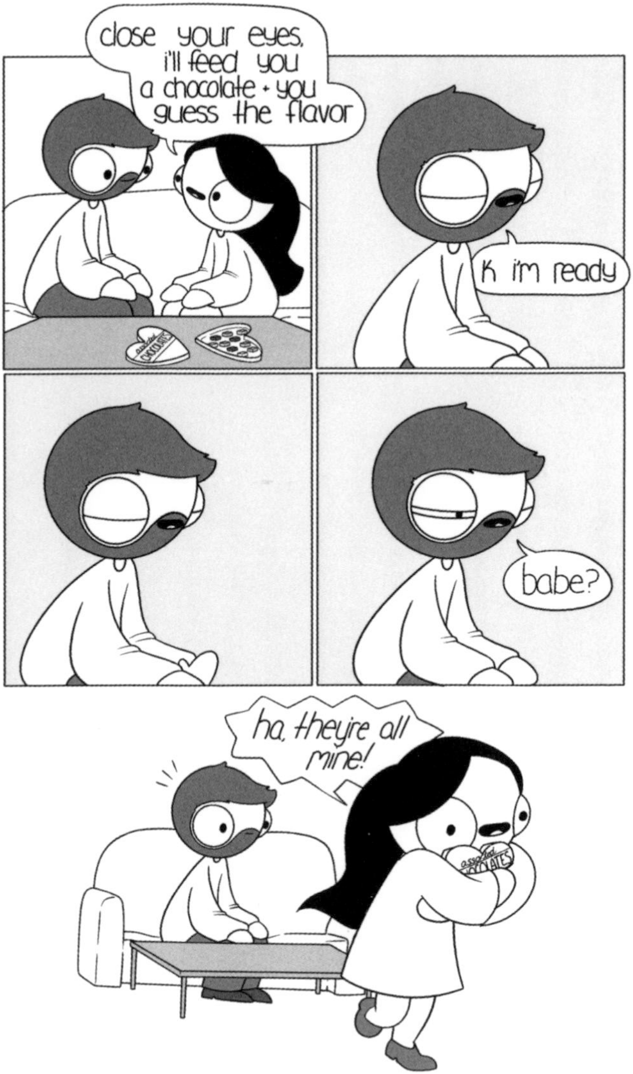
close your eyes, i'll feed you a chocolate + you guess the flavor
assorted chocolates
k i'm ready
babe?
ha, theyre all mine!
assorted chocolates

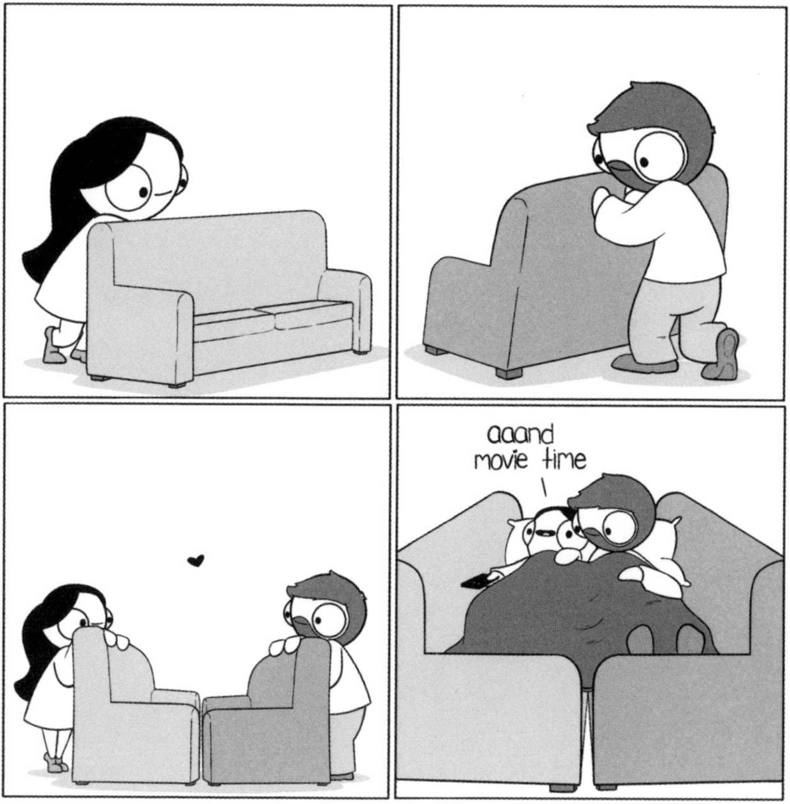
aaand
movie time

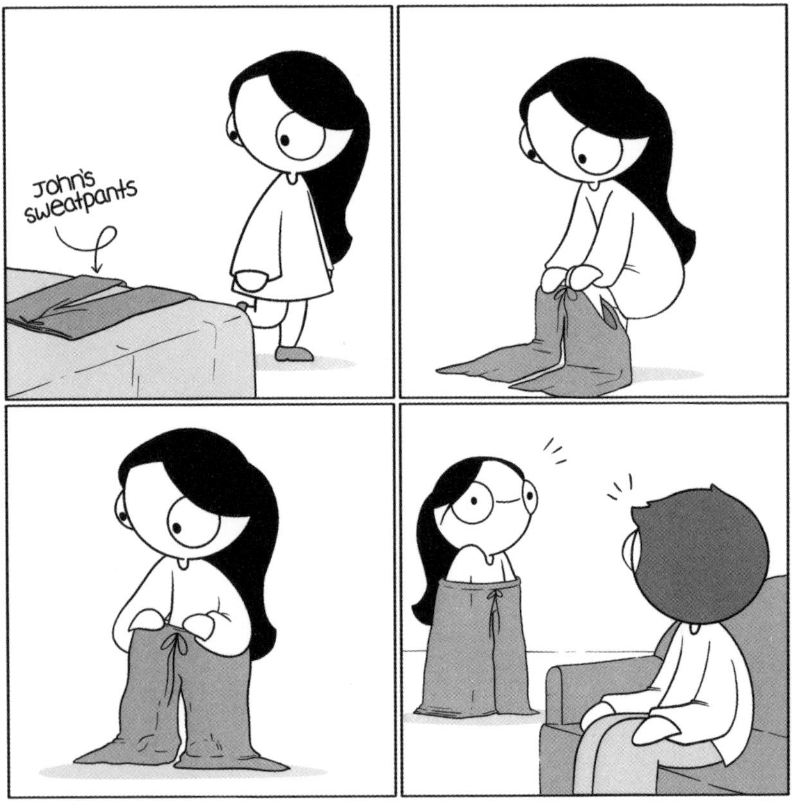
John's
sweatpants

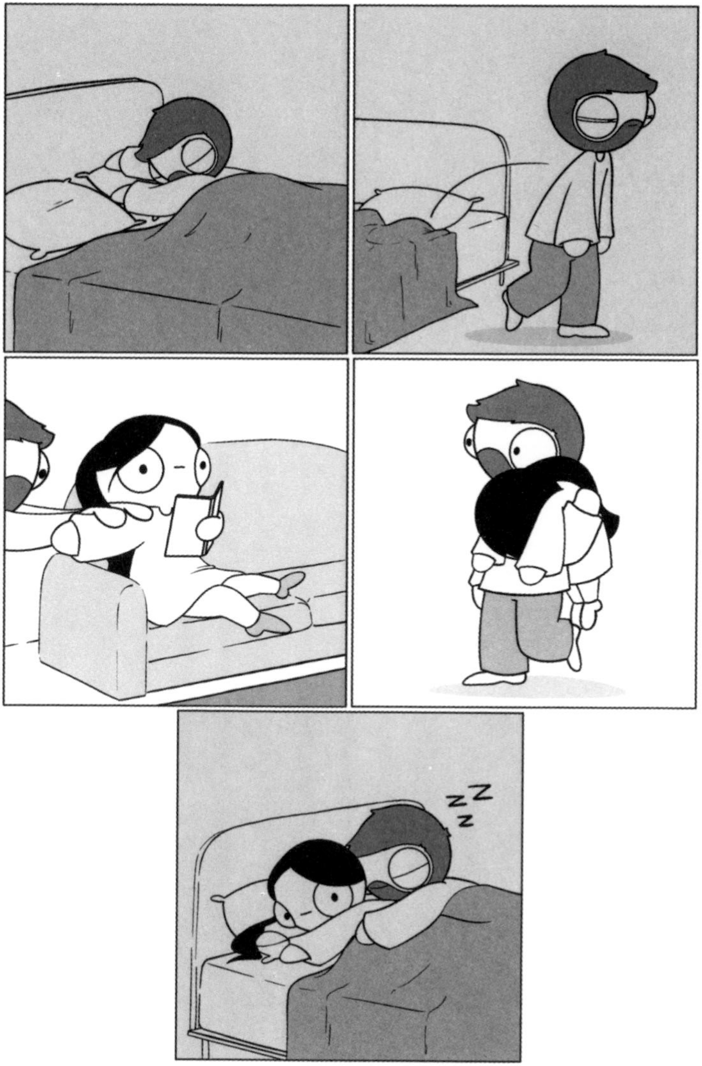
Z Z Z

— 9AM —

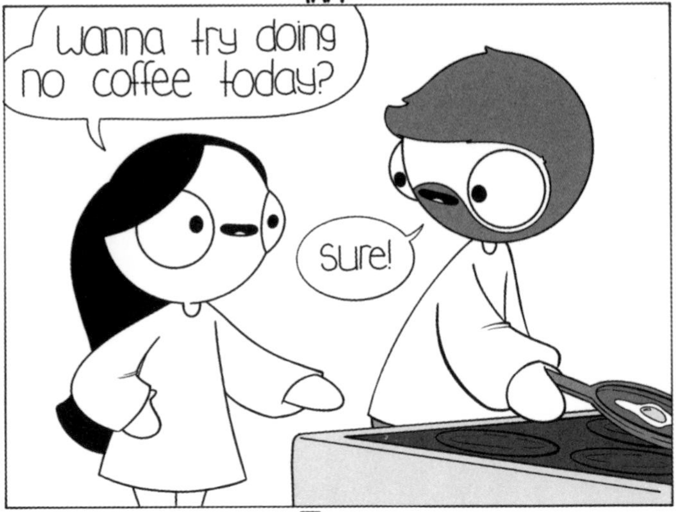
wanna try doing no coffee today?
sure!

— 3PM —

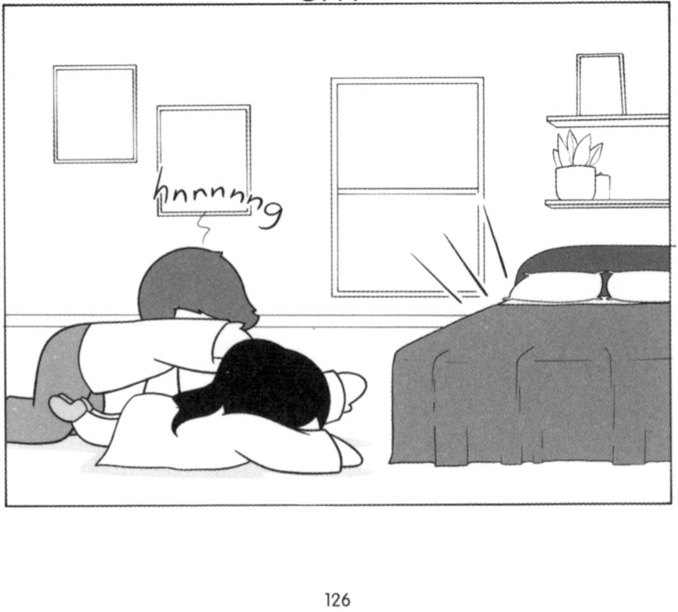
hnnnnng

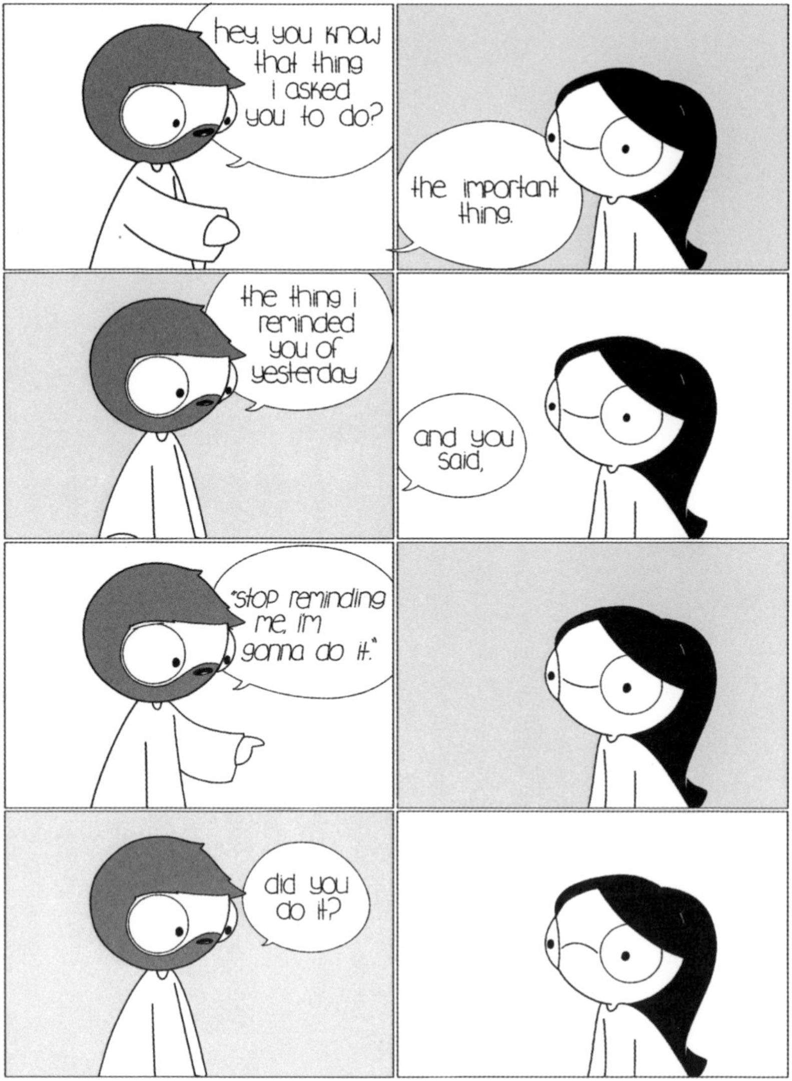
hey, you know that thing i asked you to do?
the important thing.
the thing i reminded you of yesterday
and you said,
"stop reminding me, i'm gonna do it."
did you do it?

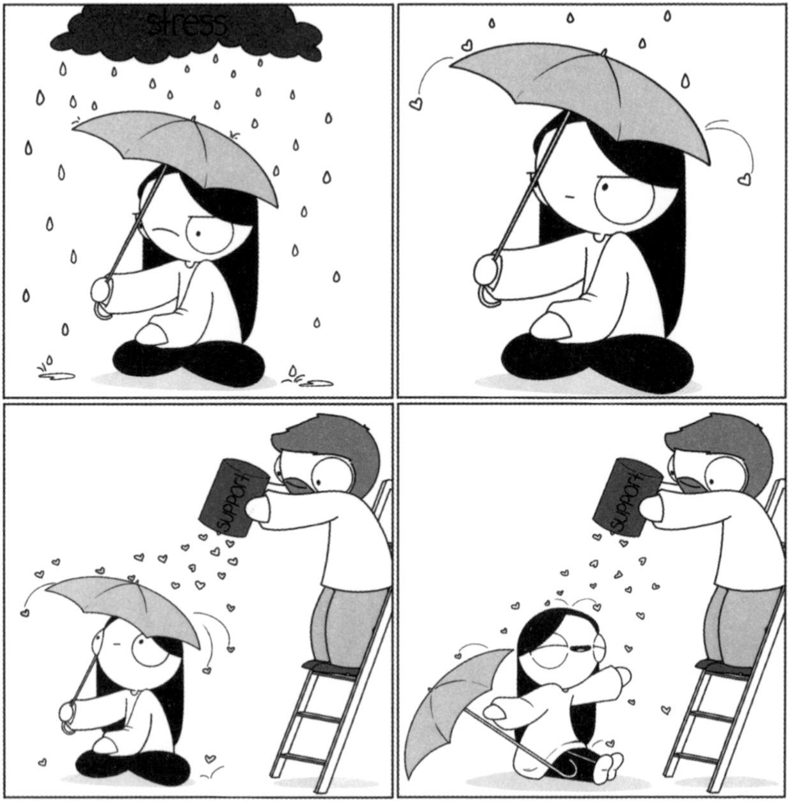
stress
support
support

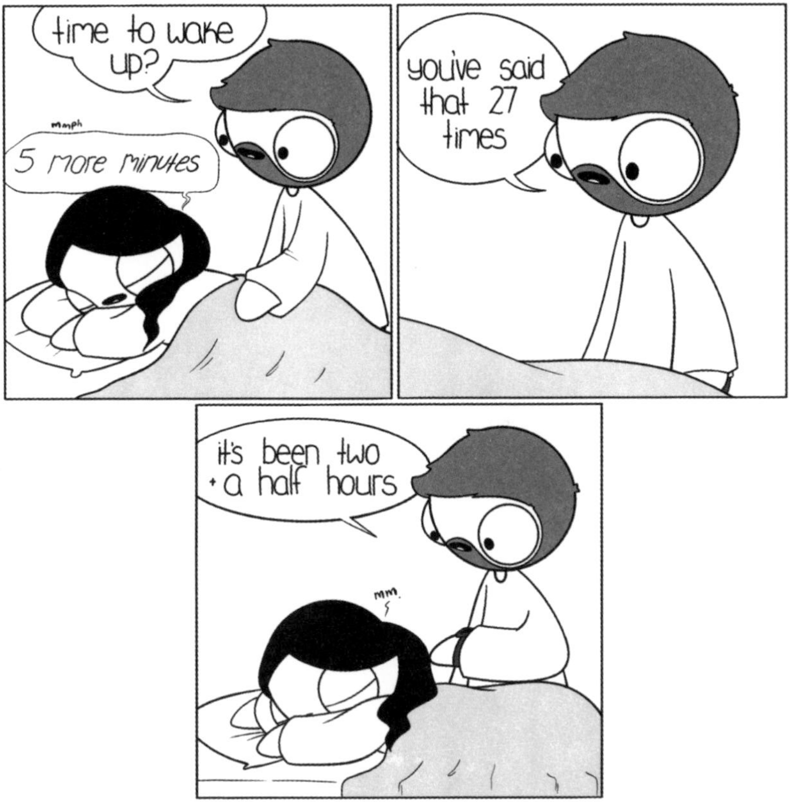
time to wake up?
mmph
5 more minutes
you've said that 27 times
it's been two + a half hours
mm.

Catana Chetwynd is a self-taught traditional artist and the enthusiastic author of *Catana Comics*. She grew up in Saratoga Springs, New York, where she spent her time creating art and pursuing an education in psychology until accidentally stumbling into the world of comics. Not only is her boyfriend, John, the daily inspiration for her drawings, but he was also the one who suggested a comic series about their relationship in the first place. Thanks to his idea and his inspiring daily antics, Catana was able to pursue her childhood dream of being a cartoonist. She currently lives on the East Coast with John and their tiny, angry dog, Murph.

Andrews McMeel Publishing
a division of Andrews McMeel Universal
1130 Walnut Street, Kansas City, Missouri 64106

www.andrewsmcmeel.com

20 21 22 23 24 SDB 10 9 8 7 6 5 4 3 2 1

ISBN: 978-1-5248-5463-8

Library of Congress Control Number: 2019947292

Editor: Patty Rice
Art Director: Holly Swayne
Production Editor: Amy Strassner
Production Manager: Tamara Haus

Attention: Schools and Businesses
Andrews McMeel books are available at quantity discounts with bulk
purchase for educational, business, or sales promotional use. For information,
please e-mail the Andrews McMeel Publishing Special Sales Department:
specialsales@amuniversal.com.

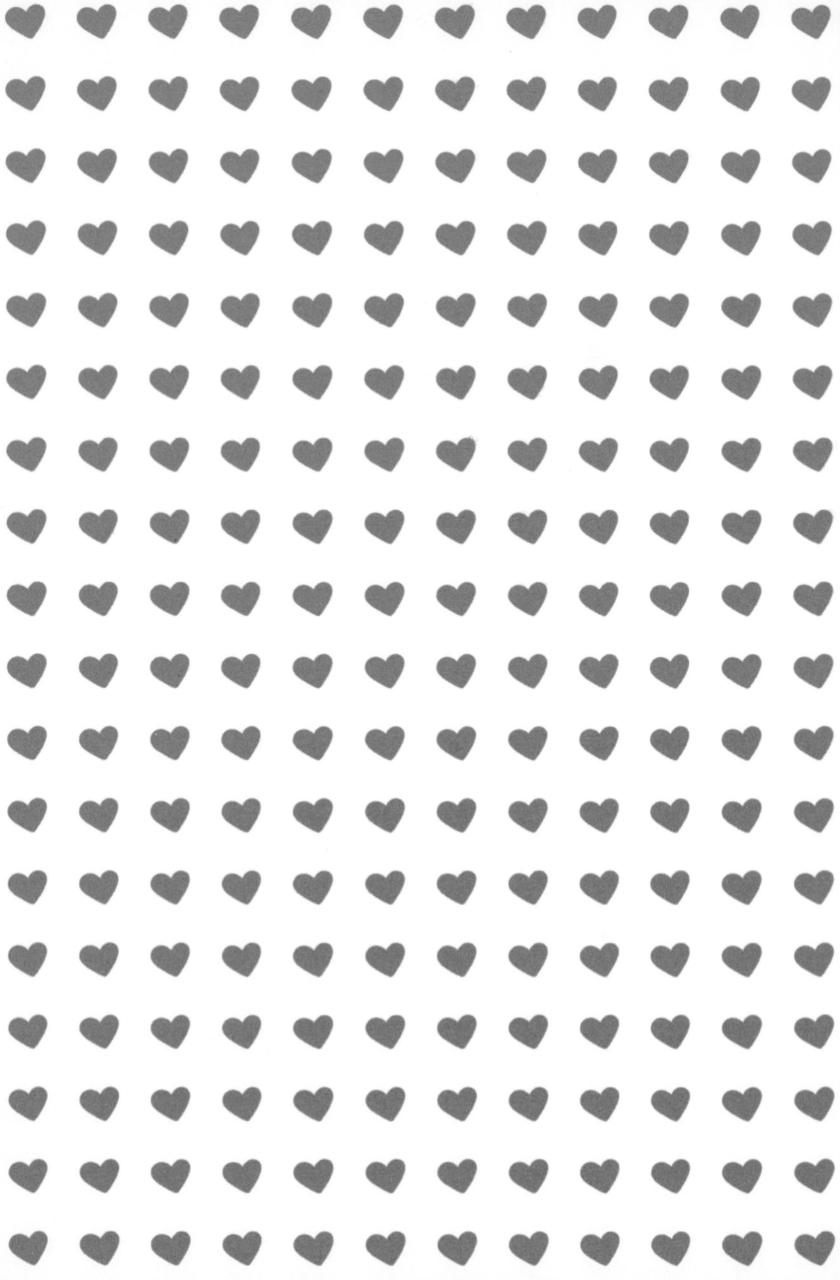